HAPPY AND GLORIOUS

DONALD EDGAR

HAPPY AND GLORIOUS

The Silver Jubilee

1977

ARTHUR BARKER LIMITED LONDON
A subsidiary of Weidenfeld (Publishers) Limited

Contents

To Rosalie

List of Illustrations

ONE

Towards the throne

Elizabeth was born on 21 April 1926, in a stately town-house at 21, Bruton Street, Mayfair, in London. Less than a fortnight later, on 4 May, a general strike started which threatened the fabric of British society. But the fabric proved very durable and the trade unions were defeated with ease in nine days. The Conservative prime minister, Stanley Baldwin, having won, avoided humiliating the losers. But it had been a serious confrontation. A whiff of revolution was in the air and troops were encamped in Hyde Park, not many yards from Bruton Street.

Elizabeth's father was Prince Albert, Duke of York, second son of King George v, King–Emperor of an empire which straddled the world. She was christened by the Archbishop of York and named Princess Elizabeth of York. The heir to the throne, the Prince of Wales, was unmarried so that Elizabeth's father was next in line. Elizabeth, as his first child, was consequently born not far from the crown.

But it was not a secure time for crowned heads and their families. Before the First World War King Edward VII had in the heyday of what was called after him, Edwardian society, sensed doom and said that he doubted if the British monarchy would last beyond his son.

The 1917 Bolshevik Revolution in Russia swept away the Romanoff dynasty and the principal members of the family were murdered. The Hapsburgs lost the crowns of the Austro–Hungarian Empire. At the end of the war the Hohenzollerns lost the German Empire. The minor royal family of Greece, of Danish–German origin, had been exiled in the early twenties; Prince Philip had been brought to safety in a British warship and was beginning his education as an exile at St Cloud outside Paris.

These events had their effect on the British royal family. The monarchies were one great family and, whether allies or enemies in war, its members were linked by blood and sentiment. In addition, the extinction of so many monarchies inevitably induced a sense of insecurity among those that remained.

Elizabeth was an attractive, healthy child. Four years later, in August 1930, her sister, Margaret, was born. The family lived in a large mansion in Piccadilly near Constitution Hill and within a few hundred yards of Buckingham Palace.

The Princesses' mother, Elizabeth, Duchess of York, was the daughter of the Earl and Countess of Strathmore.

The great quality of Elizabeth was her sparkling sense of enjoyment. Prince Albert, second son of the King, was a great match for the daughter of an Earl. But he was not very strong, somewhat shy and suffered from an impediment of speech.

He had, however, considerable qualities. He was serious-minded and was conscious of the responsibilities that came with his privileges. His wife brought him happiness and gave him confidence.

Princess Elizabeth and her sister spent a secluded childhood until 1936. It was a life of privilege rather than of luxury. There were nannies, nurse-maids, later a governess. There were visits to the grandparents – to King George and Queen Mary at Windsor, Balmoral and Sandringham – to the Earl and Countess of Strathmore at Glamis Castle in North Scotland.

Lessons were taken privately. In 1935, when Elizabeth was nine, her parents discussed with King George whether she should go to a school. The King was against it. The Prince of Wales, now forty-one, was still unmarried after turning down all the eligible princesses and daughters of the nobility. It also now seemed unlikely that the Duke and Duchess of York would have any more children. In the absence of a brother who would have taken precedence, Princess Elizabeth was growing closer to the throne.

The decision against school was hard on her. The restricted life she led as a girl did not help her to overcome a natural reserve and shyness. Beyond the nurseries, the lawns, flower-beds, stables and agreeable landscapes that encompassed Elizabeth, the years of her childhood were not happy ones for the world at large. The Great Depression, starting in Wall Street in 1929, was moving through the world like a plague, condemning millions of men to unemployment as if they, their wives and children were surplus to humanity.

Outside the capitalist world, Stalin in Soviet Russia was building a new state on, as we now know, the labour of millions of slaves, worked and starved to death.

It was an evil time, with worse to come.

The capitalist world, then, as now, led by the United States of America, was in a state of collapse. The solutions of orthodox economics were tried and failed. Keynesian economics had not yet been accepted at a high enough level. Rational thinking, found wanting, was abandoned in many countries. One carefully considered analysis put the blame on sun spots.

In the USA, when the orthodox Republican businessmen, represented by President Hoover, had failed, the Americans elected the Democrat President Roosevelt with almost dictatorial powers. His New Deal, based on a large measure of state intervention, for which he has never entirely been forgiven by American business, put the country back on its feet.

Italy had already accepted in the twenties the authoritarianism of Mussolini, a man cast in the classical role of the Renaissance *condottiere*. His policy won the support of the Vatican, which is accustomed to have the final say in Italian politics.

But, far more foreboding, the able, industrious and obedient Germans had succumbed to the evil genius of Hitler. Once more the world was to suffer from the *furor teutonicus*, with the destruction of the Jews one step on the road to world conquest.

The republic of Spain was overthrown by the forces of Fascism, led by Franco, in a war where Germans, Italians and Russians intervened and tested their new weapons and tactics on the Spanish people.

France was corrupt and without its native courage – a nation riven with dissensions between right and left.

But Britain remained stable, though there were three million unemployed and distress was widespread. A Fascist movement, led by the restless and rich Sir Oswald Mosley, eager for power at any cost, was easily put under control. A coalition, so-called national, government, controlled by the Conservatives and led by Stanley Baldwin, was overwhelmingly successful in elections. The institutions, above all Parliament and the courts of law, fulfilled their functions peacefully and the City of London controlled the economy.

The monarchy, if anything, seemed to grow in popularity. In 1935 King George and Queen Mary celebrated the Silver Jubilee of their reign. The enthusiasm with which they were greeted in their drives round London surprised and moved the King.

He died the following year on 17 January 1936. He had cared for his people in Britain and the Empire in a simple, sincere way. He did his duty as he saw it, led a life of routine and imposed a hard discipline on his sons. His heir, the Prince of Wales, found it irksome.

The Prince of Wales succeeded his father as Edward VIII. He enjoyed a phenomenal popularity, the foundations of which had been laid during the First World War when he was in his early twenties. He had been eager to share the lot of the millions serving on the western front and although the politicians and generals protected him from danger, this was not his fault. His family has a reputation for courage. It would, probably, have been better to let him share the common danger for he had brothers to replace him.

After the victory that yielded only bitter fruits for millions of ex-service-men, the Prince of Wales became their royal representative. They felt that he knew something of what they had endured and had their interests at heart.

He endeared himself to the world's women by his boyish good looks, charming smile and a certain casual diffidence. He set new styles in dress. He rode at fences and broke a few bones. He went out dancing with pretty women in public places. He represented a new mood of freedom and impatience with tradition.

He made tours abroad with overwhelming success. Even if he was a bit late at times for functions, there was nothing to forgive. He was Prince Charming. He could do no wrong.

The Americans were enthusiastic and admired his fresh, easy style. Even the more staid Canadians gave him boundless praise. For the British monarchy he was a wonderful boost at a time when many Emperors and Kings had disappeared without regret. For the world's press he was a natural. Every-thing he said or did was news.

The adulation was enough to turn anyone's head. Unfortunately his head was not too strong.

Unwilling to marry, to the annoyance of his father, he had had a few mistresses to whom he showed considerable affection. But a few years before he came to the throne he met in London an American woman, Mrs Wallis Simpson, who with her husband played a part in the smart Anglo–American set.

A slight, dark-haired and good-looking woman, she was elegant and talked amusingly. She had a great deal of what was called in those days, sex-appeal.

The Prince fell deeply in love with her.

When he became King at the beginning of 1936, events began to move fast. Her name was in the Court Circular as a visitor to Balmoral. She was acting more or less as hostess at dinners – much to the anger of Elizabeth's mother when she and her husband were invited. In the summer she went with the King on a yacht cruise along the Dalmatian coast. She was helping him to reorganize the royal palaces. She was also getting her second divorce.

The British Establishment realized, first with incredulity and then with anger, that the King intended to marry her.

The King's coronation had been fixed for 1937 and at that ceremony he would have to take the oath to uphold the Church of England of which as sovereign he was Head. The Church did not admit divorce.

But the question of divorce was only one of the reasons the British Establishment had for ensuring that if the King wished to marry Mrs Simpson, he would have to go.

Meanwhile the King was living in a dream world, hoping that all would happen as he wished. Surrounded with adulation and deference for so long, it was hard for him to believe that he could not do what he wanted.

As the crisis grew during the summer and autumn, the British public remained in ignorance of the whole matter. The newspaper proprietors, in deference to the King and the government, agreed to print nothing and a number of men and women were employed cutting out articles and pictures in American and other newspapers and magazines which arrived in this country. It was an extraordinary form of censorship which could only have happened in a Britain still governed by a dictatorial Establishment.

The Establishment at that time comprised the influential sections of the Conservative party, the City, the Church, the land-owners, the Law and the Civil Service. The families were in many cases interlocking.

While the public remained in ignorance of the situation, the men and women of the Establishment were busy talking in their clubs and drawing-rooms. They developed a savage campaign against not only Mrs Simpson, but against the King himself.

It was said that he was lazy and unintelligent; that he had become a spendthrift pouring out money and jewels on Mrs Simpson; that he was deceiving his household officials; that he was sacking valued servants at the behest of his mistress. That, in sum, he was not fit to be King.

The stories about Mrs Simpson were even more colourful. She was promiscuous, avaricious and well on the way to ruining the royal finances. She was determined to be Queen at all costs.

Mr Baldwin, with tact and some sorrow, told the King when his determination to marry Mrs Simpson was made clear, that he could not do so and remain on the throne.

The King tried to rally support too late. The censorship which he had been glad to ask for in the reporting of the divorce case of Mrs Simpson, held in the unlikely venue of Ipswich, now turned to his disadvantage. The

Establishment broke the news of 'a Constitutional Crisis' in *The Daily Telegraph* and *The Times* and the King found himself bitterly attacked. After all the years of unrelieved press adulation the King found this unbelievable. He could not understand how it could happen to him, Prince Charming.

On 10 December the King abdicated, made a dignified farewell broadcast in which he spoke of 'the woman I love', and left immediately in a warship for France. His determination to marry Mrs Simpson had won against all the inducements to stay in one of the most exalted positions which the accident of birth could give.

Elizabeth's father became George VI. She was now heir to the throne. The family moved to Buckingham Palace and were from then on surrounded by the traditional pomp and circumstance.

In spite of the crisis, the British monarchy as an institution had not been shaken. But the terms in which it functioned had been spelled out by the predominantly Conservative Establishment. To that extent it was a humiliating time for the royal family.

The new King soon won respect. There was sympathy for a man who had taken on a task for which he had not been prepared and which would tax his strength.

The former King, now Duke of Windsor, married Mrs Simpson and then lived mainly in France. But the Establishment was still revengeful. Mr Neville Chamberlain, then Chancellor of the Exchequer, wanted to take financial reprisals on the former King. Mr Baldwin, not a vindictive man, disagreed, but certainly for some time the finances of the Duke were unsettled. When he started to write highly-paid articles for the American press which could have proved an embarrassment, adequate money was made available.

There were other humiliations. It was laid down that though he remained His Royal Highness, his wife was not entitled to be called Her Royal Highness. It was stipulated that if there were any offspring, they would not be members of the royal family.

It is comparatively easy, however, not to shed tears over the Duke and Duchess of Windsor. They were honoured guests of Nazi Germany at a time when war was looming and expressed to their hosts more than polite praise. They were living in Paris when the Germans broke through in 1940. The evacuation from Dunkirk which the British had turned into a miracle had been completed. The defeat of France was already likely.

Major 'Fruity' Metcalfe, a former equerry who had devoted himself to the Duke far beyond the call of duty, went to see the Windsors when the fall of Paris was imminent.

The beginning of a life-long attachment. 'What a peerless beast a horse . . . the only serviceable courtier without flattery.' – Sir Philip Sidney.

Christmas shopping at Harrods before the war. Elizabeth & Margaret with their mother, the Queen. 'Enter a different world.'

The spring of 1944, just before D-Day. It was her eighteenth birthday and her grandmother, Queen Mary, came, wearing a touch of Edwardian finery, to wish her well.

OPPOSITE ABOVE 20 November 1947. The marriage ceremony in Westminster Abbey is over. She drives away with Prince Philip at her side.
The first touch of pageantry in war-scarred Britain for many a day.

OPPOSITE BELOW After the wedding. A view of the crowds in the Mall from Buckingham Palace where the bride and groom waved from the balcony.

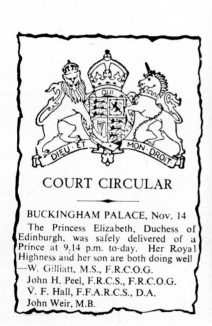

COURT CIRCULAR

BUCKINGHAM PALACE, Nov. 14

The Princess Elizabeth, Duchess of Edinburgh, was safely delivered of a Prince at 9.14 p.m. to-day. Her Royal Highness and her son are both doing well
—W. Gilliatt, M.S., F.R.C.O.G.
John H. Peel, F.R.C.S., F.R.C.O.G.
V. F. Hall, F.F.A.R.C.S., D.A.
John Weir, M.B.

14 November 1948. The first child.
A boy.

Prince Charles has been christened. Bows on her hat; a smile on her face.

OPPOSITE ABOVE 8 February 1952. Queen. The proclamation on the steps of the Royal Exchange in the city of London. The heralds wear their tabards, the aldermen their gowns.

'We do hereby with one voice and consent of Tongue and Heart publish and proclaim that the High and Mighty Princess Elizabeth Alexandra Mary is now, by the death of our late Sovereign of Happy Memory, become Queen Elizabeth the Second, by the Grace of God Queen of this Realm and of all Her other Realms and Territories, Head of the Commonwealth, Defender of the Faith, to whom lieges do acknowledge all faith and constant Obedience, with hearty and humble Affection.'

OPPOSITE BELOW June 1952. The first Trooping the Colour as Queen is over. She salutes the Household Cavalry at Buckingham Palace. Her mother and sister look down from the balcony.

DAILY EXPRESS

No. 16,517   TUESDAY JUNE 2 1953   CONTROLLING SHAREHOLDER **LORD BEAVERBROOK**   Weather: Sunny intervals, showers   Pri

BE PROUD OF BRITAIN ON THIS DAY, CORONATION DAY

ALL THIS—AND EVEREST TOO

Crowds singing in the rain

By R. M. MacCOLL
and a team of Express Staff Reporters

DESPITE the rain, defying the rain, singing in the rain, the People surged into London all day yesterday, and equally sat or lay down in its streets.

They moved in massively on the route of the Procession, with the things they would need for a wait of anything up to 30 hours, and just squatted down.

When it rained, which it did several times, they huddle under oilskins and macintoshes. When the sun came out, they came out.

There was a bit of Bank Holiday on Hampstead Heath about the crowds, a rather dreamlike quality in the sight of women snoozing on the gravel of The Mall pavements in mid-afternoon, and the motor-cars of the great stalled by sightseers.

A hoe-down

It was a colossal picnic, a hoe-down on an heroic scale. Saskatoon established squatters' rights alongside Bertram. Kalgoorlie vacuum flasks chatted with Kensington sardine sandwiches.

Concerts were started and pathetic songs were sung to the accompaniment of, here, mouth organs and, there, piano accordions.

The Mall became a vivaciously decorated camp. Under the trees there were twin lines of crazy quilting stretching all the way along, on which the dug-in pilgrims were bedding down for the night—overcoats, waterproofs, rugs, groundsheets, even bath mats.

New crowds trudged along, hovering uncertainly as people thought they spotted an unspoken-for inch or two. They picked their way among the recumbent and the sitting, among the sprawled stoves and flasks, the hard-boiled eggs and sausages.

Rumours

But the early arrivals worked our defensive tactics to ensure that they kept what they had. Human cuckoos got nowhere.

Round Buckingham Palace the seething delirium of the past weeks moved towards flash-point. Police, people, and cars seemed to be performing a complicated square dance round and about the Victoria Memorial. A swirl here, an eddy there—and then a big rush when something or someone arrived in the Palace courtyard.

Rumours sprang up and died quickly. It was on, it wasn't. The Queen. By-look-up there—that window. That, sure enough, was Prince Charles and he was not only having a good time waving down at us but also conducting a sort jig-o-war with a nurse using the window curtain as a rope.

Now there came the big cats taking away the Prince Majesty after their lunch with the Queen. But yesterday it did not matter how big and imposing was the official emblem sported by a car. The car just had to stop against a wall of people who shouted cheerfully to the occupant.

Leaping up

In the squashed, crammed laughing Mall, sleepers jerked awake and leaped and rushed forward into the roadway whenever there was anything from to see.

A girl in ballet tights jumped up and down to try to see the top of Sir Winston Churchill's head. Hurrah—here, passing along were the Queen Mother and Princess Margaret.

Now there was a huge laugh. For it tickled the crowd that the cause of a particularly big congestion was the breakdown of a Guards officer's small car.

The bowler-hatted driver jumped out and waited to push her car along The Mall until official action soon people for forward to give him a hand.

There soon twelve 30,000 or 40,000 people around the Palace, and they kept arriving.

To call a doctor

People living within the Coronation area were advised to ring the nearest, today. Special arrangements have been made for calling doctors.

Three girls made the Queen's dream dress

EXCLUSIVE!

Robb the Daily Express artist, is the only man—apart from designer Norman Hartnell—who has seen the gowns the Queen and the Royal Family wear today. It is from his drawings, and Hartnell's sketches, that the world's Press has now learned the greatest-ever fashion secret.

NOW TURN TO PAGE 3

By ROBB

THE Queen's Coronation dress—simple in style, luxuriant in detail—was made by only three girls. Six girls did the jewelled embroidery.

And when the Queen's dressmaker, Norman Hartnell, was asked what he thought of the completed dress he said just this: "I think my little embroideresses have done the finest work of their careers."

The story of the dress began last October. Hartnell was asked to submit designs.

The dress, said the Palace, must be both regal and religious. It must have no exaggerated shape because of the robes with which it would be worn.

But it must not be a simple Coronation dress like Queen Victoria's, who was only 18 and unmarried. The Queen could wear something grander.

Said Hartnell: "I sketched numerous ideas, and it was only on the eve of presenting them that I had the inspiration.

"It was that the dress should bear the emblems of Great Britain embroidered in full colour."

Her Majesty said she could wear the emblems, but the dress must also include all those of the Commonwealth.

When I first saw the dress on the stand at Hartnell's workroom I got the impression that it was made entirely of glass.

Such is the effect of the thousands of pearls, each set in its equally small saucer of silver, which entirely cover the white satin bodice and skirt.

The skirt, full and wide to the hem, breaks into full colour on the panels which carry the emblems.

First is the leek of Wales in flower, embroidered in pale green and studded with pearls and diamonds. Then follows the green shamrock of Ireland in emeralds and diamonds, and the thistle of Scotland in amethysts.

Massed round the hem in a blaze of colour are the oak-leaf for England, maple-leaf for Canada, mimosa for Australia, fern for New Zealand and other emblems, around the Tudor rose.

All are embroidered in natural colour.

When time and rain mean just nothing

CORONATION EVE. It looks like a melancholy frieze at Whatl-have-Ehold Corner, Trafalgar square.—Transparent wraps. plastic sheets, macintoshes, cover this sitting-in-the-rain team at the kerb edge—but where faces show they are still smiling.

HILLARY, 3 DOES IT

First Briton, first to reach the top

Express Staff Reporter

BRITAIN has conquered Everest, C John Hunt, leader of the British Everest expedition, announced last on the eve of the crowning of Elizabeth—that the summit of 29,002ft. Everest, highest mountain in the world, been reached for the first time—and was well.

Edmund Hillary, a 34-year-old New Zealand bachelor bee-keeper, and the 39-year-old Sherpa, "Tiger" Tensing Bhutia, climbed to the summit on Friday.

Their success came, after a month's battle against all the weapons with which Everest has repelled all previous attempts in the last 32 years—ice, treacherous powder snow, temperatures dropping to nearly 80 degrees below freezing, and winds of 30 to 40 miles an hour driving through "windproof" clothing.

Steps carved

The path of Hillary and Tensing's triumph was prepared by Wilfred Noyce, 35-year-old Charterhouse schoolmaster, who hacked a way up the steep Lhotse glacier with Angenab another Sherpa, after Noyce's other supporting men had gone down with mountain sickness.

Noyce and Annullo carving steps out of the snow-covered ice crossed what they modestly called "a very nasty" step over a deep crevasse at the top of the Lhotse glacier.

Then thus made the way for 14 Sherpa porters toiling up with 16lb. of equipment each to 26,000 feet.

The Sherpas were led by Major Charles Wylie, a 33-year-old Regular Army officer, who speaks their language and gave them the all-important inspiration and encouragement to overcome the fearful lassitude that assails all climbers in the rarefied air five miles up.

Energy reserved

With Wylie were Hillary and Tensing—coming along as fellow-travellers, reserving their energies for the ordeal that lay ahead of them.

Colonel Hunt and his men left England in February. In a "Yellow Idol" town of Katmandu they descend 300 species to carry their four and a half tons of equipment and trekked 200 miles to the base of the mountain.

It was a set-back, march. The cavalcade toiled up heartbreak ridges and down gorges through which wild rivers churned.

Lashed by rain and hail they pressed on and into a Shangri-la

PAGE TWO, COL. ONE

Police furl a Royal Standard

TWO policemen, an inspector and a sergeant, climbed to a first-floor flat in Earls Court-road, S.W. yesterday, to furl a Royal Standard which was flying from a flagpole.

The occupier of the flat, Mr. Douglas Robinson, was out. So the officers went next door and asked permission to cross from an adjoining balcony.

An official of the Earl Marshal's office said: "The Royal Standard is hoisted only when the Sovereign is in a building."

Pinza pips Aureole

PINZA, Gordon Richards's mount, is clear favourite for the Derby at 5-1. The Queen's horse, Aureole, finished a clear second-favourite at 11-2 at last night's Victoria Club call-over.

Full call-over prices on Page Seven.

Man stabbed as he dials 999

Albert Partridge, of Sunwell-street, Camberwell, S.E., was taken to hospital last night after being found with a stab wound in the lounge in a telephone box at Peck-ham-road, as he stumbled to have been dialling 999. Police detained a man later.

Princess invested

The Queen invested Princess Margaret and Princess Marie-Louise with the insignia of the Grand Cross, Victorian Order, at Buckingham Palace yesterday. The Queen also invested members of her household and the Queen Majesty received with their Coronation awards.

Razor-slasher in The Mall

A razor-slasher among Coronation crowds in The Mall last night "ripped the coat of a young girl who went on a Brabant coat asking for a needle and thread to mess to 75 guineas.

Sold out

"Sold out" was the reply from several agencies or dinners for Coronation seats last night. Even stands had seen inviting seats spirits had none to offer.

Earlier recorded prices of seats in some stands rocketed from 35 guineas to 75 guineas.

From the mums...

A sit-up-the-side car with people basking from the door had furs seated Corsica roads last night. The treasure inside a message for the mums... Afterwards mums and youngsters.

Nehru: Swiss trip

BERNE, Monday. The Indian Prime Minister, Mr. Nehru, will preside over a meeting of Indian diplomats in Europe at Burgenstock, Switzerland, on June 13.—Reuter.

In the front line again. A privileged position for the Chelsea Pensioners. It rained heavily – just as it did on the morning of Waterloo.

A night to remember. Sleeping out – but not so rough with rugs and thermos flasks.

OPPOSITE Coronation Day – 2 June 1953. The headline that summed it up.

The Coronation Medal.

'How sweet a thing it is to wear a crown.' *Henry VI, Part III*. On the way to Westminster Abbey to be crowned.

One of the Coronation drives. They wheeled the patient out for a successful operation.

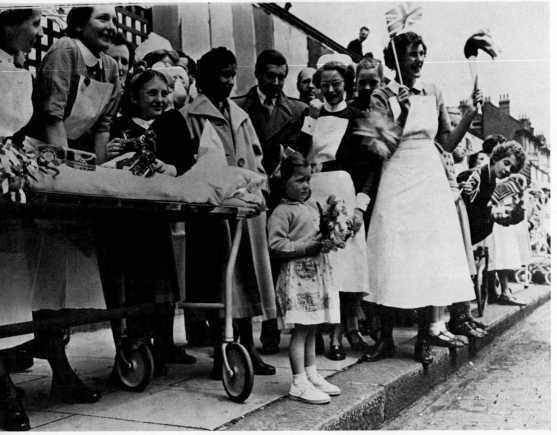

Even his loyalty and patience broke when he found them concerned more with the fate of the Duchess's wardrobe than the peril of Britain and their adopted country, France.

The Windsors reached safety in Portugal. By courtesy of the Germans, the Duchess's maid was given a safe conduct to collect the clothes left in Paris. That there were German special envoys attempting to establish links with the Duke is fact. It may be that Hitler thought that if his invasion of England was successful the Duke and Duchess might be useful as puppet King and Queen. But nothing came of the German diplomacy. Even more important, nothing came of the German invasion.

The Duke made many requests to Winston Churchill, now prime minister, for useful employment. They were something of an embarrassment and Churchill had at that time many more vital problems on his hands. Fortunately, however, an opportunity arose when he could send him to the Caribbean as Governor of the Bahamas.

After the war the Duke and Duchess settled in Paris and with trips to New York and the South of France became admired members of a smart international set, living lives of luxury and futility.

In May 1937 Elizabeth, who was then eleven, had her first experience of the ceremonial splendour of monarchy. Wearing a train of purple velvet and a gold coronet she attended her father's coronation in Westminster Abbey and was made conscious of her public importance.

Her parents were now away more often on official visits. The pattern of her life was still a routine of lessons and play, but inevitably she was now the centre of much attention. She was a conscientious pupil, acquired a good French accent, but a dislike of mathematics. The Provost of Eton gave her history lessons. She rode ponies and played in very large gardens with her sister and a few other children chosen from her parents' friends.

The world was moving towards war. Hitler occupied the Rhineland with impunity in 1936, then incorporated an enthusiastic Austria into the German Reich and in 1938 dismembered Czechoslovakia. This last act did nearly lead to war, but Britain and France negotiated an agreement at Munich which for a time raised false hopes of peace.

Italy had completed her conquest of Ethiopia, in spite of half-hearted sanctions imposed by a League of Nations which had now lost all authority.

Britain was at last re-arming and stock-piling food and materials. This created economic activity and the unemployment figures started to fall.

Mr Neville Chamberlain, who had succeeded Mr Baldwin as prime minister, and negotiated the Munich agreement, enjoyed the support of most Conservative MPs. Winston Churchill thundered warnings largely unheeded although he had some adherents, among them Anthony Eden and Harold Macmillan.

The Labour party, led by Mr Attlee, was hamstrung by its policy of pacifism. Left-wing opinion was being built up in the country by the brilliant Labour lawyer politician, Sir Stafford Cripps, with the help of the Left Book Club, a publishing venture founded by Victor Gollancz which soon broadened into a Socialist movement.

In Great Britain at this time five per cent of the population owned seventy-nine per cent of the wealth; one per cent owned fifty-six per cent.

In the spring of 1939 Hitler marched into the remains of Czechoslovakia, wrecking the hopes of Munich. For many that summer had the poignancy of farewell.

The King and Queen, with Elizabeth and Margaret, visited the Naval College at Dartmouth in the royal yacht, *Victoria and Albert*. The occasion had a significance. War was imminent and the Royal Navy, the senior service, was still the symbol of British power. It was also the King's service.

Among the senior cadets was Prince Philip, then eighteen. He met the royal family and talked to Elizabeth, then aged thirteen. It was their first meeting.

While a British military mission was vainly trying to reach an agreement in Moscow, Stalin made a deal with Hitler. Thus protected, Hitler attacked Poland. Britain and France declared war.

The King and Queen shared the dangers of London during the war. Elizabeth and Margaret spent most of their time at Windsor. They were subject to food and clothes rationing and the other wartime restrictions.

In the autumn of 1940, after the fall of France, an invasion of Britain was likely. There was talk of the royal family going to Canada. If Britain was occupied, it could symbolize across the Atlantic the Empire's determination to carry on the war.

The answer was given by the Queen. She said that her husband had no intention of going. That this meant she had no intention of going. And that where she was, the children would be.

Elizabeth followed the course of the war. She read the newspapers and listened to the radio. She met young officers back on leave.

When she was eighteen she put on uniform and did some training as a junior officer in a woman's army transport unit. It taught her something about the inside of a car or lorry. The photographs taken and published had a good effect – probably, as much as anything, on herself. She was doing something.

Victory in 1945 was a time of conscious pride in Britain. For the Dominions and most of the Empire it was a time for rejoicing. For France and the other occupied countries it was an end to privations and humiliations. For the United States it was the end of a considerable task which she had, with her illimitable power, taken in her stride. For the people of Russia and Eastern Europe it meant the agony of the Stalinist tyranny. For defeated Germany it meant a country divided between East and West; occupation, hunger and pride humbled in the ruins of its cities. For Japan total humiliation in the ashes of nuclear fall-out.

Britain had earned wide praise for standing alone in 1940, but the end of the war found her in a desperate condition financially and economically. Her foreign investments had been sold. Vast debts had been incurred abroad. Her transport and machinery were worn out. There were few exports to pay for food and raw materials. Rationing and shortages were inevitable for years ahead.

TWO

Emergence of a monarch

After the defeat of Germany, the coalition over which Churchill had presided was broken up. In a general election the Labour party, led by Clement Attlee, decisively beat the Conservatives with a promise to lay the foundations of a welfare state.

In 1945 the day of scientific opinion polls had not dawned and the extent of the victory surprised even the Labour party. Churchill, misled by his advisers, had been confident of victory.

The King knew the principal members of the new administration. They had been members of the wartime coalition government. Clem Attlee, Ernest Bevin, Herbert Morrison, Sir Stafford Cripps, had all held high office and were as experienced in running the country as the members of any former government.

To an outside observer it may have seemed an example of the providence that guards the destiny of the British. A policy of radical change was to be carried out by a group of men tried and tested in the difficult years of war.

Wartime experiences had played a large part in deciding the election of a Labour government. There had been hardship and suffering, but the mass of the British people had also become aware of new horizons promising a better life.

The war of 1939–45 was for Britain a people's war to a much greater degree than that of 1914–18. Every fit man and woman of adult age was liable to conscription. If they were not in the services, they were in the mines, factories and offices or on the land. All classes had to accept draconian powers over their labour and resources such as were not imposed by Hitler in Germany until the closing phases of the war.

The bombing of Britain, though it did not amount to more than a fraction of the fury launched later on Germany by the allied air forces, was severe enough, especially in the large cities, to give a sense of involvement in the physical dangers of war.

The men who had served overseas came back with a changed outlook on life. The battles which the British fought, though on a great scale, had not caused the mass slaughter of the trench warfare of 1914–18. In this more open war, covering many countries and several continents, there were opportunities to look around and to think. The British soldier, mixing to a certain extent with Australians, New Zealanders, Canadians and South Africans could not but be aware that these men were superior, not necessarily in courage, but in physique, education and standards of diet. Class attitudes and accents did not seem to divide them. These men from the Empire, largely of British stock, looked at the world as if they were masters of their environment, not its servants.

For women, too, the pattern of pre-war life fundamentally changed. Hundreds of thousands were drafted into the armed services, finding themselves subject to discipline and, within the discipline, free of family responsibilities and constraints. On the land and in factories it was the same story. For millions of women the husband or boy-friend was absent for years on service. Many of the traditional sex taboos seemed irrelevant.

In addition, hundreds of thousands of Americans and Canadians were stationed in Britain. These servicemen needed female company and sex if they could get it. Sometimes the relationship was casual and greedy on both sides; sometimes deeply felt and treasured for a lifetime. But these Americans and Canadians brought not only their youth and their dollars. They brought a breath of fresh air, of self-confidence, of a way of life that made the girls and women realize the relative misery, for most, of pre-war British life.

In 1945 a majority of the British people felt a better life was within their grasp. They voted for the party they thought would give it.

For the British monarchy the election of a government of radical change has always had its problems. However loyal to constitutional monarchy, governments of reform have tended to erode the residual political powers of the sovereign. But, with some understandable initial reluctance, British monarchs have shown great skill in adapting to reforming governments such as those led in the past by Liberal leaders – Gladstone in the nineteenth century, Campbell-Bannerman and Lloyd George in this century.

But the Labour government of 1945 was more than a reforming administration. It was determined to change the structure of the country's economy.

Mr Attlee ended his career as an Earl and a Knight of the Garter, but he was a socialist, albeit a believer in gradualism. Though himself a member of the upper-middle class, he gave high office to men such as Aneurin Bevan, of working-class origin and a man who wanted to sweep away as much of old privileged capitalist society as he could, as quickly as he could.

The problem for the British monarchy is that it is very rich and is surrounded for the most part by men and women who are also rich and privileged.

Princess Elizabeth was nineteen in 1945. For her the war had been restricting in some ways, but had also given some opportunities she would not have had in peace-time. Even in the royal circle, class and financial barriers had been breached.

She had also been made increasingly aware of her position as heir to the throne, for her father's health was failing. The Palace officials wisely encouraged her to take an interest in events at home and abroad.

Emotionally this was an exciting time for Elizabeth. Prince Philip, who had visited her when on leave, had found a secure place in her heart. They corresponded and his photograph was in her room. Her parents looked with a fond eye on the developing relationship.

Philip had many suitable qualities. He was of the right age, five years older than the Princess. He was handsome, intelligent and had had a good war career. That he had no money of his own was not of importance to a rich family. He was also a Prince and the number of eligible Princes had dwindled. Probably, if Elizabeth had found a suitor she loved in one of the noble families of Britain, it would not have mattered that he was not royal. But a Prince is a Prince. It was undoubtedly a mark in Philip's favour that his family was related to that of Elizabeth.

Philip's uncle – his mother's brother – is Lord Mountbatten, who is related to the royal family. By 1945 he had established himself as a war leader of heroic proportions with victories gained and disasters endured. From the early years of the war when his destroyer, HMS *Kelly*, was sunk off Crete, he had risen to high command, ending as 'Supremo' of the allied forces in South-East Asia. He took the surrender of the Japanese at Singapore. The ceremony, conducted with icy formality, did something to redeem, in the eyes of the world, the humiliating unconditional surrender in 1942.

He has demonstrated that, even in the twentieth century, a man of princely blood can shine by personal efforts.

In 1946 the relationship between Princess Elizabeth and Prince Philip had deepened. By all accounts, it was in the romantic country around Balmoral, where Victoria and Albert had found great happiness, that they decided they would like to marry.

Her father suggested a delay, partly to give her time to make sure in her own mind, partly because there were many to consult about the marriage.

A royal visit to South Africa had been arranged for the spring of 1947 and Elizabeth was to accompany her parents and sister. It was decided to wait until the tour was over before making a final decision.

The South African visit was important. The original settlers, mainly of Dutch origin, had been defeated by the British at the turn of the century in the so-called Boer War, one of the more disreputable chapters in the story of British imperialism. Since then the British had poured in, attracted by the wealth of gold and diamonds. But the old colonists, now called Afrikaners, did not forgive or forget.

A nationalist party grew up which was dedicated to the renewal of Afrikaner power. Many of its leaders hoped for a victory by Nazi Germany and were imprisoned for acts of sabotage. The Afrikaners were also fundamentally opposed to the British liberal attitudes towards the social and political development of the black and coloured population.

The royal visit was intended to help unite the Afrikaners and British in a common purpose within the framework of the Commonwealth.

The royal family sailed in the battleship *Vanguard*, which Elizabeth had launched in 1944. It was a splendid adventure for Elizabeth and Margaret to sail in a great ship, surrounded with the disciplined care of the Royal Navy on their first ocean voyage.

The scenery she saw in South Africa widened Elizabeth's horizons. The dimensions of the veldt and the rivers dwarf the landscapes of Britain. She also found herself in a country where black and coloured people predominated.

The South Africans of British origin gave the royal family a great welcome; the Afrikaners unbent. The mission of the King and Queen failed, however; the nationalists soon secured lasting power.

Elizabeth had her twenty-first birthday during the tour. She reviewed a parade of troops, accompanied by Field-Marshal Smuts, originally a Boer leader who had become an elder statesman of the Empire. It was he who had pressed for the visit.

In the evening there were two balls and Elizabeth was surrounded by much loyalty and affection. But the lasting effect of the day was the radio broadcast that Elizabeth made to the Empire, directed at her own generation.

She studied the words carefully and finally knew them just about by heart. They sank in. They were a message for her. 'If we all go forward together,' she said, 'with unswerving faith, a high courage and a quiet heart, we shall be able to make of this ancient Commonwealth, which we all love so dearly, an even grander thing – more free, more prosperous, more happy and a more powerful influence for good in the world – than it has been in the greatest days of our forefathers. To accomplish that we must give nothing less than the whole of ourselves.

'I declare before you that my whole life, whether it be long or short, shall be devoted to your service and the service of our great imperial family to which we all belong.'

Soon after the return from South Africa, Princess Elizabeth's engagement to Prince Philip was announced. In fact he was no longer a Prince. He had become a naturalized British subject and renounced his titles as Prince of Greece and Denmark (where the Greek royal family had come from). There was a problem about his surname. At one time there was talk of giving him the name 'Oldcastle', an English translation of Oldenburg where his family had ancestral connections. Finally, it was agreed that he should be Philip Mountbatten, taking the name of his mother's family. It represented an agreeable increase of prestige for Lord Mountbatten.

Princess Elizabeth and Prince Philip were married at Westminster Abbey on 20 November 1947. Philip had been made a Royal Highness, Duke of Edinburgh, Earl of Merioneth, Baron Greenwich and a Knight of the Garter.

The wedding took place with a pageantry that had been missing for a long time in Britain. The bride looked beautiful, the groom handsome as they drove through the streets in a refurbished coach, escorted by Household Cavalry with waving plumes and highly polished cuirasses. The Guards were back in ceremonial red tunics and bearskins. There were cheering crowds outside the Palace as the couple appeared on the balcony, although it was not a festive time in Britain. The immediate joy of victory had passed and there was not much to celebrate. Rationing was still severe. Material shortages made recovery difficult. Russia, only yesterday the wartime ally, was now a dangerous threat.

The marriage was a popular event and evoked much affection and loyalty. The first part of the honeymoon was spent at the elegant country-house of the Mountbattens, Broadlands, in Hampshire.

A few years followed which were, as near as possible, idyllic for Elizabeth. She and Philip paid a visit to France in the spring of 1948, and even those difficult friends, the French, gave a warm welcome. Prince Charles was born on 14 November 1948, and Princess Anne on 15 August 1950. They were fine, healthy children. Philip was serving as a naval officer in the Mediterranean with headquarters at Malta, since the days of Nelson the symbol of British power in the area. Elizabeth made as many visits there as possible and the couple lived a free-and-easy life in the sunset glow of the island's role as a British base. There was quite a family atmosphere. Lord Mountbatten was there and Philip himself had his own naval circle. Elizabeth and Philip made one visit which meant a great deal to him. It was to Greece where the royal family of which he was a member was enjoying one of its popular spells and the hardships of Nazi occupation and cruel civil war against the communists were giving way to a degree of prosperity.

The outstanding visit of this period was, however, to Canada in the autumn of 1951. Aside from traditional loyalties, the British monarchy has one great advantage there. Canada is wide-open to the influences of the United States, especially financial, but is steadfastly independent of spirit. The monarchy provides a link with Great Britain and the other countries of the Commonwealth which in a quiet, dignified way asserts that independence. Elizabeth and Philip were attractive representatives of that link. The size of the task ahead became obvious to her. The spectacles of the Canadian scene from the Atlantic to the Pacific were breath-taking.

She made a good impression in the province of Quebec, that island of people of French origin that resents being submerged by the Scots and English that dominate the country.

To make the path even easier for Elizabeth in Canada, the Governor-General of the day was Lord Alexander of Tunis, a famous wartime leader of armies and a handsome, cultivated member of the British aristocracy.

Elizabeth and Philip took the opportunity of paying a call on President Truman in Washington. They were only in the United States for two days, but the visit was important. Apart from Anglo–American links it was only with the massive aid of the Marshall Plan that Britain and Western Europe were able to re-build their shattered economies.

At the beginning of the next year, 1952, Elizabeth and Philip set off by air for a long tour of East Africa, Ceylon (now Sri Lanka), Australia and New Zealand. Her father, the King, waved good-bye. He looked a sick man.

A few days later while Elizabeth was watching wild-life in East Africa, news came through that her father had died in his sleep during the early morning of 6 February.

She was the Queen and twenty-five years old.

THREE

Settling in

The prime minister who greeted the new Queen at London Airport the following day was Winston Churchill. The Conservatives had won the general election the previous October. Churchill was in his late seventies, rather deaf, often rightly worried about his health, but still magnificent on the big occasions. His task was to maintain what he could of Britain's dwindling power. In this he suffered humiliations, especially in Washington. But he shrugged them aside and battled on, throwing his personal prestige into the scales.

In Churchill the Queen had a prime minister who revered the throne. Lord Moran in *The Struggle for Survival* wrote: 'The House of Lords means nothing to him. The history of England, its romance and changing fortunes, is for Winston embodied in the royal house. He looked at a new photograph of the Queen. She was in white, with long, white gloves, smiling and radiant. "Lovely," he murmured, "she's a pet. I fear they may ask her to do too much. She's doing so well."'

In the field of domestic politics, the main structure of the Labour government's social edifice remained undisturbed. The nationalization of the basic industries, the policy of full employment, the health service, improved education and more and better houses – all were accepted with few reservations by the new government. The new society was, in fact, developed by Churchill's colleagues, notably Harold Macmillan and Rab (later Lord) Butler.

The first months of Elizabeth's reign were a challenge to her. But she was young, healthy and surrounded by a devoted staff. There was the routine of her job to master – the fascinating task of reading daily the ministerial boxes which provide her with the gist of all important developments; consultations with her officials; the weekly meeting with the prime minister; audiences to British, Commonwealth and foreign diplomats; programmes of functions and a large mail, even when sifted by her staff.

She was also head of a large household of several hundred and finally responsible for the royal finances, both public and private.

Being a woman, the question of clothes was important. As Queen she would need more, and of a different style.

Financially, 1952 was a difficult year for Britain. New restrictions were imposed on the supply to the home market of consumer goods, including cars. The annual foreign travel allowance was cut from £100 to £25.

The Conservative elder statesman, L. S. Amery, started off the year in a letter to *The Times*: 'Nothing short of the most drastic measures can avert national bankruptcy and the break-up of the sterling area before the end of 1952.'

Britain exploded her first atom bomb in an attempt, that then seemed possible, to remain in the front-rank of powers. The development costs had been skilfully hidden from public scrutiny in the budgets of Mr Attlee's government.

General Eisenhower, who as American commander in the West was well-known in Britain, was elected President of the United States.

Britain's Comet, the first jet passenger plane in the world, started to fly and was a source of national pride. In 1954 after several crashes it was found to have disastrous design faults and had to be withdrawn from service until they were corrected. A vital lead was lost.

The Korean war in which America had faced Chinese Communist forces was coming to an end in a sullen armistice.

It was announced that the coronation would take place on 2 June 1953 and that television cameras would be in Westminster Abbey.

In March 1953 Stalin died and the man who had defied him and survived, Marshal Tito of Yugoslavia, came to London and was given lunch at the Palace by the Queen.

The Queen's grandmother, Queen Mary died, aged eighty-five. A woman with the dignity and presence of a vanished age, she had been a patron of the arts. In later years her love of beautiful objects had led to the embarrassing habit of pocketing pieces she admired in the houses of her friends or the shops she visited. Sorting out the problems became a major task for her staff.

The government managed to produce an easy budget in the spring and preparations went ahead with a will for the coronation. Stands were put up in the streets. Souvenirs were mass-produced. Decorations were designed ranging from great triumphal arches to humble home-made affairs – 'Long Live Our Liz.' There were flags and bunting galore.

Winston Churchill was made a Knight of the Garter. There were rehearsals of the ceremony in the Abbey which were conducted by the Duke of Norfolk, who being hereditary Earl Marshal was in charge of the whole affair. Representatives of the world media came to augment Fleet Street and Broadcasting House. The Duke instructed them in a series of conferences which he addressed with authority and a humorous charm that captivated his audience.

The day was to be a public holiday. Sugar, meat, bacon and fats were providentially to be freed from rationing.

The leaders of the Commonwealth arrived.

The Queen was given lunch in Westminster Hall by 750 representatives from fifty-two Commonwealth legislatures.

Hotels were taken over to house the distinguished guests who were coming from all over the world. Private visitors found it difficult to find accommodation whatever the price.

The elaborate celebrations in London were reflected in every city, town and village of the country. Events were organized for children, old people and hospital patients. Oxen were prepared for roasting whole on village greens. The brewers and distillers could not deliver enough of their products.

The knights of the orders of chivalry hired their ceremonial costumes which had been in mothballs since the last spectacular historical film. Tiaras were brought out of bank vaults. The members of the House of Commons, Conservative and Labour alike, preened themselves in their court dress, knee breeches and silk stockings.

It was as if the whole country had gone slightly mad.

When the day came, it was, 'All This And Everest Too', as the *Daily Express* proclaimed. News had come through that a team led by Colonel (later Lord) Hunt had climbed the highest mountain in the world. Edmund Hillary, a New Zealander, later knighted, and Sherpa Tenzing, were the first men ever to set foot on the summit. It had been a challenge to the British for many years. Previous attempts had cost lives. It is difficult now, when the mountain has been climbed many times by many nations, to appreciate that everyone in the country took pride in the achievement.

It rained heavily on coronation day, making it uncomfortable for the thousands of troops and police and the hundreds of thousands of spectators on the route.

But millions of the people of Britain sat in front of television sets in their homes or in bars and restaurants (the number of sets was still limited) and watched the ceremony in Westminster as it happened. This is what made the coronation of the Queen unique.

Television had in those days the advantage of being new and slightly miraculous. It is, consequently, not surprising that the coronation has remained in the memories of those who watched it as a special, unforgettable day.

The coronation is a ceremony of great splendour and beauty in which the sovereign, church and nation perform a ritual of symbolic union. On this occasion when the monarch being anointed and crowned was a young woman, visibly conscious of its significance, it was natural to be moved.

In a broadcast the Queen said: 'I have behind me, not only the splendid traditions and the annals of more than one thousand years, but the living strength and majesty of the Commonwealth and Empire, of societies old and new, of lands and races differing in history and origin, but all, by God's will, united in spirit and aim.'

That evening was celebrated with gusto and the British, as is their custom on a solemn occasion, laughed and drank and made ribald remarks to hide any emotion they may have felt. What had it meant to them? Probably an increased sense of national unity and loyalty. If so, the whole elaborate affair had justified itself.

The next morning *The Times* warned in a leader entitled, 'And After?': 'The British people have had a holiday from reality long enough. . . . Even in a welfare state facts must be seen penny plain. Britain's economy still sways on a knife edge. . . . A country made great by resourcefulness and energy is slowly strangling itself with restrictive practices [and] by a plain disinclination for hard work.'

The coronation celebrations went on happily for weeks. At Spithead the Queen reviewed two hundred ships of the Royal Navy. There was a fly-past of three hundred aircraft of the Fleet Air Arm. The navies of the world sent ships to honour the occasion – including the Russians.

There was a review of the RAF with six hundred aircraft and a display of its thirty-five years of history.

The Queen and Prince Philip made tours of London and throughout the United Kingdom.

That was coronation year. Memorable. Though the memories may now be tinged with sadness.

It was in confident mood that the Queen and Prince Philip set off in late November 1953 on their six-months' world tour of the Commonwealth.

They needed every scrap of confidence. The Empire had begun its difficult metamorphosis into a Commonwealth of free countries. India and Pakistan had become independent in 1947 and although they joined the Commonwealth, there were faint-hearts in Britain and ill-wishers abroad who doubted whether any association would succeed the impending dissolution of the Empire.

Concerning the condition of Britain itself, the world had been told since the end of the war of a battered and exhausted country embarking on a perilous social policy which would destroy the fabric of its old institutions.

The influence of monarchy had also been eroded, partly because the royal family had not been able to make many visits since the beginning of the war. A new generation was growing up even in the countries peopled with British stock to whom the monarchy might seem a remote and unnecessary tie, incompatible with mature nationhood.

The task of the Queen and her husband was to restore and strengthen faith in the future of the British connection.

They flew first to the West Indies, which were in a few years to become independent within the Commonwealth. It was an easy start, for the West Indians are generous of heart and have a natural love of pageantry. They turned the visit into a carnival of music, flowers and laughter.

The royal party boarded the liner, *Gothic*, which had been chartered for the next long stage. They went through the Panama Canal and sailed into the Pacific.

Those were halcyon days for the Queen. She was twenty-seven, sailing across the Pacific with her husband in a liner converted luxuriously for her use, escorted by ships of the British and Commonwealth navies, and on her way to visit great countries in three continents which acknowledged her as Queen. It was a voyage the like of which had never happened before – and will never happen again.

Their first calls were at South Sea islands which were part of the Empire. The luxuriant scenery, native dances, open-air feasts, gave a sense of heightened living. There was still the mysterious magic that Herman Melville described and Gauguin painted, in spite of the increasing havoc of Western materialism.

As the *Gothic* sailed through the Pacific to New Zealand and Australia, the Queen was passing through the waters which had witnessed the stupendous American war of retribution against Japan. A war of merciless killings on the islands and the greatest naval battles in history fought by fleets of aircraft carriers which rarely saw their opponents.

New Zealand and Australian troops had fought the war alongside the British in the Middle East and the Mediterranean. But in the Far East their countries had been defended by the shield of American power. The Queen was consequently visiting two countries of the Commonwealth where American influence was now strong.

In New Zealand the Queen found herself among a people of British stock with an admixture of Maori blood that has brought talent and toughness. She made an extensive tour of the country and spent Christmas there. The New Zealanders, radical in politics, have created for themselves a pleasant life. The population has been deliberately kept small. Their loyalty to the British connection seems almost a matter of instinct, overriding personal advantage. Her reception lifted the Queen's heart.

In Australia the Queen found a different people giving a warm, but different, welcome. Able, adventurous, mocking, they can assume an attitude of rude toughness to hide a sensitivity that is their closely-guarded secret. The stock is British, but since the war has been extended to Mediterranean people, such as Italians and Greeks. When the Queen paid this visit it looked as if Australia might soon come under the wing of the United States, politically and financially.

The royal party sailed on to Ceylon (now Sri Lanka), Aden and then to East Africa. They visited Uganda, then a colony, and flew on to Libya and visited Tobruk, scene of heartening victories and humiliating defeats during the Desert War. In the harbour lay the new royal yacht, *Britannia*, with Charles and Anne on board.

Britannia had just been completed. She is a magnificent vessel, 413 foot long, manned by a picked crew of twenty-one officers and 258 ratings of the Royal Navy. She replaced the worn-out *Victoria and Albert*. There has been some justified criticism of the expense of *Britannia*. The decision to build her was made by the Labour administration soon after the war, partly as an act of thanks to King George VI.

She cost originally £2¼m. She probably costs now around £2m a year to keep in commission. Her royal duties are on average between sixteen and seventeen weeks a year. *Britannia* has also been used, perhaps unwisely, for the honeymoons of Princess Margaret and Princess Anne. But *Britannia* has undoubtedly given value on state and official visits as a symbol of British maritime traditions and the world-wide extent of the Commonwealth.

Had the tour been worthwhile? There was no doubt about the welcome the Queen and Prince Philip had everywhere. They were a young, attractive pair and the crowds were delighted to turn out and cheer. That in itself was of positive value when reported worldwide in print and film – not least back in Britain.

Australia and New Zealand, the countries of mainly British stock, have remained in the family in spite of their growing sense of nationhood, their divergent trade developments and the British entry into the Common Market. It is impossible to say how significant in this respect the Queen's first tour there was. Certainly it helped.

Inspecting a camel unit of the Aden Protectorate Levies.

On the Rock of Gibraltar. The Barbary apes have been there longer than the British.

OPPOSITE ABOVE LEFT With King Idris of Libya at Tobruk.

OPPOSITE ABOVE RIGHT Melbourne. Driving away from the reception at Parliament House.

OPPOSITE BELOW With all aboard HMAS *Australia*; flagship of the Australian Navy, off Cairns, Northern Queensland.

ABOVE The Maori heritage of New Zealand. Coming away from the old Meeting House preserved at Whakarewarewa.

LEFT A guard of honour of splendid Torres Strait Islanders in Parramatta Park, Cairns, the most northern town visited in this Australian tour.
One of the guard is *hors de combat* – it has been known to happen on Horse Guards Parade.

RIGHT The Lord Mayor's ball at Sydney.

BELOW Au revoir. The crowds on the breakwater at Fremantle were one of the last sights of Australia on this first tour there.

LEFT Craftsmen show their wares. They have inherited a great tradition.

The *Durbar* at Kaduna. Part of the cavalcade that came to greet the Queen.

Oba Adeniji the Second brings forward a reluctant girl with a bouquet.

LEFT On Deeside near Balmoral. The ghillie watches the cast with a professional eye.

BELOW Near Ascot. An unexpected bonus for the tourists in the coach.

LEFT At the coal-face. Where the black diamonds come from.

OPPOSITE BELOW The Horse Trials at Badminton, Princess Margaret advising on the cine-camera?

OPPOSITE ABOVE The hounds greet Prince Charles when his mother took him to a meeting of the Eridge Hunt in the Sussex village of Hadlow Down.

A question of form at Epsom, 1958.

Good reason to smile. Lester Piggott, then 21, standing on the right, has won the 1957 Oaks for the Queen on Carrozza.

FOUR

The prosperous years

The Queen and Prince Philip had a great welcome home when in May 1954 they sailed up the Thames in *Britannia* to anchor at London. A few days later at a lunch given at the Mansion House the Queen said of her tour: 'You do not – and I know you never will – lack the friendly comradeship of the other nations of our Commonwealth family.'

Britain was prosperous and Mr Macmillan as Housing Minister was able to report that the 1953 target of 300,000 new houses – considered impossible – had been surpassed.

In Kenya the Mau Mau movement was spreading murder and terror. British troops were having great difficulty in tracking down the insurgents.

Dr Roger Bannister became the first man to run the mile under four minutes.

At the end of November there were great celebrations for Churchill's eightieth birthday. In Westminster Hall representatives of the nation paid him honour and a portrait by Graham Sutherland, one of the few outstanding artists of his generation, was presented. But Sir Winston, an artist himself, actively disliked the painting and even in his speech of thanks made everyone realize it. He had it relegated to a lumber room.

It was expected that even he would now soon retire. He did on 5 April the following year and Sir Anthony Eden, so long the crown prince, came into his own. The evening before he resigned, Sir Winston and Lady Churchill gave dinner to the Queen and Prince Philip at 10, Downing Street. In giving the toast to 'Her Majesty the Queen', Churchill reminded her that he had drunk the same toast in the reign of her great-great grandmother.

Following in the steps of the United States and Russia, Britain prepared to make H-Bombs.

At the end of May 1955 a general election was called and the Conservatives came back with a slightly increased majority.

This year the emotional crisis through which the Queen's sister, Margaret, had been passing came to a head.

The Princess and Group Captain Peter Townsend, an equerry appointed by George VI, had fallen in love. His marriage, like so many during the stresses of the war, had broken down. He was obtaining a divorce.

Margaret was a beautiful young woman, with a more dramatic personality than her sister. She was intelligent and artistic. The two sisters had been brought up together. They loved each other in the normal, instinctive way. But, inevitably, as Elizabeth grew up, the attention of the world was given to her, first as heir to the throne, then as Queen. In addition, Elizabeth had married the man she loved, who, as it turned out, was acceptable to the family and the nation. He had the added glamour of being a wartime naval officer. Loyal as Margaret may have been, it was hard for her not to feel somewhat neglected.

Peter Townsend, handsome and charming, had particular glamour as one of the heroic band of young pilots who had fought the Battle of Britain in 1940 in the skies over South-East England, preserving their country and giving the world its first proof of the British will to fight and win. The survivors were and are justly honoured. It was to honour them that George VI appointed Peter Townsend to his household.

It is easy now to say that Townsend should never have encouraged either his own desires or hers, as he was older, in a position of trust, and knew that a divorced man could not be considered as a husband for a royal princess. It is easy to say now that Princess Margaret, seeing the way her emotions were developing, should have confided, say, in her mother, if not her sister, so that an immediate separation could have made the parting easier.

It is comparatively easy when you are not young and in love to be cool-headed about a relationship. It is damnably difficult when you are young and very much in love.

The first semi-public awareness of their relationship was at the coronation. After the emotionally and physically exhausting ceremony the royal procession came into the Annexe which had been built as a huge withdrawing-room for the main participants. It was for the royal family a moment of relaxation after a considerable ordeal. Margaret and the handsome equerry could not help showing their emotion as they greeted each other. It was nothing flamboyant but there were many looking, including some journalists.

The news soon became public. Margaret was sent away with her mother on a tour of Rhodesia. Townsend was sent to Brussels as Air Attaché.

But neither Margaret nor Townsend gave up without a struggle. Townsend talked to the press in Brussels and in London. He was cool and calm. He greatly impressed the reporters who were endlessly questioning him.

But the real pressures were on Margaret. Townsend was there, waiting for her. It was for her to make the decision.

In all the accounts both then and after, perhaps there have been too few expressions of sympathy and pity for her in those weeks – and since.

As a background to the atmosphere in the Palace were memories of the Duke of Windsor, who had not so many years ago abdicated to marry a divorced woman.

Sister, mother, friends of the family, state dignitaries, archbishop and bishops – Margaret faced serried ranks of opposition – an opposition, even if expressed with sincere sympathy.

On 31 October 1955 she issued a statement saying that she had decided not to marry Townsend – 'Mindful of the Church's teaching that Christian marriage is indissoluble, and conscious of my duty to the Commonwealth, I have resolved to put these considerations before all others.'

The British press told most of the story as it happened. There was no censorship as at the time of the abdication crisis.

Townsend went on to make a prosperous career, mainly abroad, and married a charming Belgian girl. They have five children. His book on the Battle of Britain is considered a classic. He has remained silent on the whole Margaret affair.

Britain in 1955 was doing well. 'Never before,' said the prime minister, 'has the average family enjoyed so high a standard of living.'

There was a shortage of labour in many areas. Manufacturers and financiers were prospering in the domestic market catering for the new 'consumer society'. Motor-cars, television sets, refrigerators, cookers, were being bought on an unprecedented scale with the help of hire purchase. Towards the end of the year inflation began to be worrying. Sir Anthony said: 'At home we are trying to do too many things at once. This is better than trying to do too little, but it is straining our resources and raising our costs.'

Mr Attlee in December decided to retire and accepted the Earldom which it has been customary to offer to a former prime minister at the end of his career. He was succeeded as leader of the Labour party by Mr Hugh Gaitskell, who combined the cool intellect of Winchester with a passionate belief in social justice.

This year the Queen was painted by Pietro Annigoni, the Italian artist, who had made a reputation with his warm, but classical portraits of beautiful women. The Queen has been painted many times, but the Annigoni, commissioned by the Fishmonger's Company in the City of London, has proved the most successful. It shows her at her best, as a woman, and as Queen. Photographic copies have made it known throughout the world.

The Suez crisis dominated the latter part of the year, but earlier there were other significant events.

At the end of January 1956 the Queen and Prince Philip went to Nigeria. The length of the visit – three weeks – emphasized the importance of this vast country, both as a potential leading force in the new Africa and as an influential member of the Commonwealth.

In Russia, Mr Kruschev had emerged as the new leader and had denounced Stalin at the Twentieth Soviet Communist Party Congress. He was searching for a new approach in foreign as well as domestic policy and came to Britain in April with his closest colleague, Marshal Bulganin.

The visit had a special flavour. The heavy cruiser in which they arrived at Portsmouth was of interest to our intelligence services. A frogman, Cmdr Lionel Crabb, was sent to examine the hull of the warship and never returned. Kruschev and Bulganin stayed at Chequers, visited Oxford, listened to question time in the House of Commons, found themselves in heated argument with some members of the Labour party, especially Mr George Brown, and went to the ballet at Covent Garden and saw Fonteyn dance.

The Queen and Philip gave them tea at Windsor Castle and later Mr Kruschev sent a Cossack pony to Prince Charles.

This year the Queen started giving informal lunches to around ten or a dozen men and women who had achieved distinction in their widely varied careers. She has continued to give around four a year. They have been one of the most successful innovations she has made. The guests have felt honoured and the Queen has had her experience widened.

Mr Macmillan, as Chancellor, put through some anti-inflationary measures and told the nation in a broadcast that since the war production had increased by twenty-five per cent and that it had paid itself eighty per cent more for doing so. It was still easy to sell in the home market, increasingly difficult to sell abroad.

In October the Queen opened the world's first large nuclear power station at Calder Hall in Cumberland. Britain was investing massively in a nuclear power programme, which it was hoped, vainly, would solve her energy problems.

In the theatre a major new playwright appeared. John Osborne with *Look Back in Anger*, started a new chapter in British drama by presenting the post-war generation as it was. The impact was phenomenal.

At the end of October the Russians began to crush an uprising in Hungary. Mr Kruschev's thaw was soon frozen.

The Suez adventure of the autumn of 1956, when Anglo–French forces invaded Egypt, caused the most serious crisis that Britain has undergone during the Queen's reign – so far. It deeply divided the nation, cutting across party loyalties. It split the Commonwealth. It caused a rift with the United States from which the old 'special relationship' has never fully recovered. It was the last episode of British imperialism. As the implications of its failure became clear, the Tory party, then in power, shed its remaining illusions of Empire. The crisis demonstrated with clarity that, even when in alliance with France, Britain could no longer implement a foreign policy contrary to the wishes of the United States and that when, as in this case, the United States found themselves acting in concert with the Soviet Union against Britain, she faced only humiliation.

It marked the supremacy of the two super-powers, bluntly and harshly.

The illusions of Empire, however, were not the prerogative of Conservatives. Throughout the country there were many who were angered by what they considered the American betrayal when Britain attempted to assert her interests in the Middle East. The Canal was not just a stretch of useful water. It was an emotive concept, symbolic of British imperial rule. During the war millions of British had served in Egypt. To them the Egyptians were a third-rate nation of 'wogs'.

But Mr Gaitskell, leader of the Labour opposition, found widespread support in attacking the Suez adventure as a crime and a folly.

For the Queen it was a nerve-wracking time and Philip was not at her side. Through the documents sent to her, through the regular meetings with the prime minister, Sir Anthony Eden, and through the information provided by her officials, the Queen during 1956 knew very well what was happening. It was not a pleasant story.

Britain at the time still had the appearance of being the dominant foreign influence in the Middle East although American power was growing in the oil-states and elsewhere. General Nasser, the Egyptian leader, was a man of ability and great magnetism, who became a symbol not only of Egyptian aspirations, but of Arab nationalism in many countries.

Only recently the British had finally and reluctantly withdrawn their troops from the Suez Canal base.

Nasser followed this success by nationalizing the Canal (26 July), then considered a vital international waterway, which was owned by the British Government and French interests. At this stage Sir Anthony Eden seemed to lose patience with Nasser.

The French, further along the Mediterranean, were engaged in an increasingly bitter war with the Algerian independence movement which was supported by Nasser.

The Israelis, pinned down behind frontiers impossible to defend, were eager to be involved in a war which would improve their position.

The plot to deal with Nasser, hatched in many meetings, some secret, during the summer of 1956, between the British, French and Israelis was morally discreditable. Incidents between Israel and Egypt were to be provoked. The Israelis were to attack through the Sinai Desert towards the Canal. Britain and France were to land troops at Suez on the grounds that they were bringing peace and order to a troubled area.

The press knew quite a lot of what was going on. But not the full story.

After many delays, the Israelis attacked and the British armed forces moved into action in the first week of November in conjunction with the French. The RAF destroyed the Egyptian air force, mainly on the ground. The navy escorted the armada which brought in the troops. The army, led into attack by British and French parachute troops dropped the previous day, achieved their primary objectives and then, a few hours from occupying the Canal, was halted.

Whether Brigadier (later General) Mervyn Butler should have put a deaf ear to his radio instructions as Nelson put a blind eye to his telescope at Copenhagen, will remain a matter of argument. But his orders were peremptory. The reason why the commands were peremptory was that the United States, backed by the United Nations, and actively assisted by the Soviet Union, had demanded that the Anglo–French forces should halt and declare a cease-fire.

Within a few days a United Nations force took over from the British at Suez. It was humiliating for the British troops – especially as one of the first ashore was an Australian officer.

In London there were turbulent demonstrations against the invasion. Trafalgar Square, traditional scene of protest, was filled with angry shouting crowds who could no doubt be heard in the Palace, a mile away along the Mall.

The pound was attacked by the Americans to bring Britain to heel.

President Eisenhower, a few days away from the end of his re-election campaign, was angry with the British government and made it known.

Many Commonwealth countries were against the adventure. Canada's prime minister opposed it but later did his best to help Britain pick up the pieces.

There was dissension in the Foreign Service, especially among those with experience of the Middle East who saw Britain throwing away Arab good-will, earned over many years.

In the following January, two months after the landings, Sir Anthony Eden's health failed him and he resigned. He was succeeded by Harold Macmillan, who had been Chancellor of the Exchequer.

The crisis passed. Britain and the Commonwealth showed themselves extraordinarily resilient. The pound recovered.

The rift with the United States remained.

Harold Macmillan quotes a letter, known to him only years after, sent at this time by Sir Winston Churchill to President Eisenhower. It was sent without the knowledge of Westminster or Whitehall, but a copy was sent to the Queen – an example of the extent of the confidential information she acquires. 'Whatever the arguments adduced here and in the United States for or against Anthony's action in Egypt,' Churchill wrote, 'it will now be an act of folly, on which our whole civilization may founder, to let events in the Middle East come between us.'

The Queen has the right to warn her government, as well as to be consulted and to encourage. It would be interesting to know if she exercised the right during the Suez crisis.

According to Kenneth Love in *Suez – The Twice-Fought War*, she was wholeheartedly opposed to the Suez adventure for fear the operation would wreck the Commonwealth.

FIVE

Public problems, private pleasures

In February 1957 Mr Macmillan, the new prime minister, went to Bermuda to see President Eisenhower to try and repair some of the damage created by Suez. His meeting was of some benefit.

On 16 February the Queen was re-united with Prince Philip after his four month voyage in *Britannia* without her. They met at Lisbon, where they began a state visit to Portugal.

Prince Philip had during his tour opened the Olympic Games at Melbourne and visited various remote parts of the Empire.

But his long voyage, following several other tours on his own, caused considerable speculation in the American press. There was talk of a rift in the marriage.

A certain importance was attached to the reports after its early and accurate account of the Edward VIII abdication crisis. Nor was the British press silent this time. The Queen had done her best in her Christmas broadcast ... 'my husband's absence at this time has made me more aware than I was before of my own good fortune in being one of a united family'.

Prince Philip's position, though brilliant to the outside world, was not an easy one for him.

He is a man of great energy and ability, who finds it difficult merely to do his essential public duties with grace and charm and then relax with friends. His desire was to emulate the success of his uncle, Lord Mountbatten, but in his position as the Queen's husband it was an impossible ambition.

Brought up in exile mainly by relatives, who generously watched over his career, he proved himself outstanding at Gordonstoun, as a cadet at Dartmouth and in the Royal Navy. He also became increasingly conscious of his ability.

When he married Elizabeth he wanted to give of this ability largely, not only to her, but to Britain. He studied the life and works of Prince Albert, Queen Victoria's consort, whose talents, culture and desire for perfection had done much for Britain in the mid-nineteenth century. However, the monarchy Philip married into no longer had such sway in governing the country. Nor was Elizabeth unprepared for Queenship as her predecessor had been. She was not a woman to be dominated. She was always conscious of her own destiny and responsibilities and therefore less likely to be influenced by him in matters of statecraft.

Initially, like Albert, Prince Philip began to re-organize the royal households, seeking to make improvements in the way the staff were used, bringing the organization up to date after the war shortages, especially in the field of communications. His manner caused some ill-feeling amongst a traditionally devoted staff.

But Philip rapidly discovered that his study of Albert had been irrelevant. His desire to be of assistance led him to make comments which were critical of British manufacturers and selling methods. There may well have been truth in some of what he said, but it was not a field he should have ventured into as an inexperienced critic. Business expected praise and encouragement from the monarchy.

Despite his dynamic patronage of sporting activities and many organizations, including his own Duke of Edinburgh Awards, a sense of frustration was inevitable. For him these activities he patronized so successfully were sidelines rather than fulfilment of his potential.

His position at court is, to a certain extent, isolated. He does not make friends easily and has found in sections of the royal circle a similar cool atmosphere to the one Albert suffered from. His foreign extraction, energy and constant lecturing of the British seemed somewhat distasteful to the traditional attitude of muddling through.

Almost immediately on the return from Portugal the Queen conferred on Philip the style and titular dignity of a Prince of the United Kingdom of Great Britain and Northern Ireland. It was the highest honour she could give him.

The budget gave concessions to the surtax payers, which made the Government's more prosperous supporters happy. It was announced that it was hoped to end conscription, introduced in 1939, by 1960 and create a small, highly professional army, which was the service most affected.

The Queen and Prince Philip made a state visit to France in the spring. But the most important royal tour this year was to Canada and the United States.

In Canada, which had disapproved of Suez, the Queen made a television broadcast and delivered a speech from the throne at the opening of Parliament.

The original reason for the American visit was to see Williamsburg, the eighteenth-century capital of colonial Virginia, which had been carefully reconstructed. But a trip to Washington was organized. One of the functions was a banquet given by John Foster Dulles, the American Secretary of State, whose attitude to Britain, never warm, had become actively hostile during Suez.

The Queen went on to New York and addressed the General Assembly of the United Nations. It could be said that the Queen had done her best this year to rebuild the broken bridges.

Not all the Queen's social occasions were, happily, so involved with matters of state. It had been announced that the days of formally presenting debutantes at the Palace were about to end. They were not regretted, except by those ladies of aristocratic lineage who had made a business of presenting girls, mainly American.

However, in June the Queen and Prince Philip attended one of the last great debutante balls which for splendour of scene, nobility and fame of guests and lavishness of hospitality could rank as a memorial to a vanishing custom.

Americans paid for it, as they have paid for so many relics of British history, including the site of the Battle of Hastings.

The ball was for Daphne Fairbanks, daughter of Douglas Fairbanks jnr, a film star of renown who had become a notable member of Anglo–American society in London. For his wartime services to Britain he had been awarded an honorary knighthood.

The scene was Cliveden, the riverside palace on the Thames belonging to the Astors who had brought from America in the early years of the century great wealth and talent that soon made them one of the most influential families in Britain.

Princess Margaret and the lovely Princess Alexandra, daughter of the widowed Duchess of Kent added to the royal glamour. There were the Dukes of Northumberland, Bedford, Argyll, Marlborough and Rutland to head the list of the aristocracy. But the Fairbanks, with their film and theatrical connections, enhanced the occasion with handsome men and beautiful women of professional talent.

The flowers were magnificent. The food and drink lavish. The most fashionable dance-band of the day, led by Paul Adams, was there to play the most fashionable numbers of the day.

The elaborate gardens of Cliveden sweep down in terraces to the Thames. At midnight there were fireworks, illuminating the river, trees and meadows.

The Queen and Philip stayed until 3.30 in the morning when the June dawn was near.

The Queen and Prince Philip were young and the British liked to see them enjoying themselves. They were good times for most – even if it was, Live now, pay later.

Elizabeth had her stable of racehorses, zealously studied form and went to the meetings. Philip played polo with zest and yachted with skill. They went to the theatre, the 'Crazy Gang', film premieres, parties and dances.

There were plenty of light-hearted occasions to match the solemn events – Trooping the Colour, the Garter ceremony at Windsor, opening Parliament at Westminster, receiving state guests.

In spite of Suez, in spite of warnings about inflation, the mood of the nation was euphoric. 'The Chelsea Set' of the day symbolized an attitude.

They were young, often attractive, sometimes well-connected, generally able to come by spending money – and determined to enjoy themselves. Tomorrow would not come. They were probably the last example in Britain of a privileged, irresponsible youth.

At the beginning of 1958 the Russian leaders, President Voroshilov, Mr Kruschev and Mr Bulganin sent New Year's greetings in warm terms to the Queen, her family and her people.

In the Middle East, the Suez adventure had its inevitable consequences, presaging the end of British hegemony in the area. Britain's ally, King Feisal of Iraq, was murdered and the country became a republic with Communist help. The Americans, anxious to take over from the British, responded to the Russian interventions and landed troops, including a tactical atomic division, at Beirut. Jordan, then a British client state (but not for much longer), asked for help and troops were flown in from Cyprus, at the time a British colony.

In Cyprus itself the Greek section of the population, led by Archbishop Makarios, had been for some years in rebellion, demanding union with Greece (Enosis), in spite of a large Turkish minority. At one time nearly

30,000 British troops were involved in maintaining law and order – an impossible burden, especially as its former strategic purpose had disappeared with the loss of the Suez Canal.

In London there were ugly race riots at Notting Hill Gate in which attacks were made on coloured people, mainly post-war immigrants from the West Indies. There were similar riots in Nottingham. Arrests were made and heavy sentences passed.

The immigration of hundreds of thousands of coloured people principally from the West Indies, India and Pakistan and of Asians, no longer welcome in the newly independent states of East Africa where they had originally been settled as a willing labour force, has been a major factor in the life of Britain throughout the Queen's reign. Entry has now been made difficult, but by 1978 there will be two million non-white citizens in the country and they tend to have larger families than the whites.

Their integration has taxed the resources, the imagination and many traditional attitudes of the country.

For years after the war coloured immigrants were encouraged to come to Britain to fill jobs that the whites, having a choice under full employment, did not wish to take.

If Britain could achieve a harmonious integration, it would be one of her greatest triumphs, with considerable benefits in the future as the coloured peoples of the world achieve power and influence.

But as the Queen sees with her own eyes on any of her tours of this country, the ethnic structure has changed. The problem is a testing one.

For the Queen it is significant for she is head of a Commonwealth that is to a large extent not white. She is fortunate that her judgment on the problems in Britain has been matured by her visits to many countries where white is coloured.

In October the West German president, Dr Theodor Heuss, came to London. The state visit passed off very well, considering the past. It was the first time since 1907 that a head of the German state had visited London officially. West Germany had rebuilt its economy with miraculous speed after the war and was now playing a vital role in the defences of the West. To the Germans the visit marked another step forward in their rehabilitation.

At the end of November 1958, the Commons debated the Wolfenden report on homosexuality and prostitution which had been published the previous year.

This presaged 'the permissive society' in Britain, which has given form to the changes in thought and behaviour in many of the most profoundly important spheres of life.

Abortions have been made legal. Divorce no longer relies on the so-called guilt of one of the parties, but is granted when a marriage has broken down. Homosexuality is permitted among consenting adults. Censorship has been abolished in the theatre and, virtually, in films and books. Street prostitution has been more or less extinguished by the creation of a call-girl system.

The development of the oral contraceptive has probably changed the lives of women more deeply than anything in history. Its implications are still largely unknown. But, certainly, the British birth-rate is falling phenomenally.

Marriage as a civil or religious ceremony is still a normal practice, but cohabitation is so widespread that any social stigma is fast disappearing. Illegitimacy is ceasing to have a meaning, except in the case of inheritance – and moves are ahead to make changes there.

The movement for equality between the sexes has won nearly all its battles. Nothing less than a new society is being created.

In 1959 Marlborough House, in the Mall near the Palace, was handed over by the Queen for use as a Commonwealth centre. It had in more spacious days been traditionally the home of the Prince of Wales of the day and was now a costly white elephant. The prime minister said that eventually provision would have to be made for a London home for the Prince of Wales. Taking into account the extent of royal accommodation already available, this caused raised eyebrows among even staunch monarchists.

Cyprus was given its freedom, but not union with Greece. It elected to be a member of the Commonwealth.

Fidel Castro, a left-wing nationalist, took power in Cuba from a corrupt repressive regime. Mr Nixon, then vice-president of the United States, went to Moscow. This followed an earlier visit by Mr Macmillan. Mr Kruschev in the autumn spent a fortnight in the United States.

The Queen spent six weeks in Canada and opened the great St Lawrence Seaway jointly with President Eisenhower. He in turn visited Scotland in August and paid a visit to the royal family at Balmoral. There was a picnic on the shores of a loch with Charles and Anne accompanying their parents.

Opening 'stately homes' to the public was becoming big business. Lord Montagu of Beaulieu and the Duke of Bedford, two of the most lively noble entrepreneurs, showed that hundreds of thousands of visitors could be entertained with pleasure and profit. Gradually most of the great houses were opened and millions of visitors, including many tourists from overseas, came to observe the past glories of the country-house privileged way of life and the new attractions of zoos and lion safaris. In a curiously English way, this development had a social, almost political, value. Noble families found a new function and the grandeur of architecture, pictures, furniture and grounds were admired by millions whose forbears would probably have only entered as servants.

The first British motorway was opened. Roast beef was still the traditional Sunday meal in one-third of all homes – a tradition soon to be priced out.

Mr Macmillan – 'Supermac' to the cartoonists – held an election in the autumn and the Conservatives came back with an increased majority. The Macmillan slogan 'You've never had it so good' has since been criticized even by his own party for its cynical optimism. But, in fact, for most people life was reasonably good. Unemployment was low, money easy to raise and prices fairly stable.

Keynesian economics – vulgarized into the slogan, 'When in trouble, a touch of inflation works wonders', were fashionable not only in London. They set the tone in Washington. At the time they seemed to work splendidly.

SIX

Wind of change

In 1960 Mr Macmillan went to an Africa struggling to be free and bravely made his 'Wind of Change' speech in South Africa, firmly dedicated to apartheid, 'We must not take too gloomy a view; these are exciting days for Africa.' They were. The Congo was in turmoil after the Belgians precipitately left. But Nigeria, one of the largest and richest British colonies, became independent in October, peacefully, and joined the Commonwealth.

In South Africa this was the year of the Sharpeville and Langa shootings in which eighty-three non-whites were killed and 365 wounded by police bullets. It was a result of a non-violent campaign against the pass regulations. Over twenty thousand Africans were arrested.

The Queen gave birth to a second son, Prince Andrew, on 19 February.

General de Gaulle paid a state visit and was given very special treatment including a ceremonial military parade and a splendid firework display. The crowds cheered him as the leader of the French Resistance who had made his headquarters in London. But the visit did not change his deep-seated hostility.

Princess Margaret married Anthony Armstrong-Jones in Westminster Abbey with all splendour on 6 May. There were the largest crowds on the streets since the Coronation.

Armstrong-Jones, who was created Earl of Snowdon the following year, came of a family of distinction and had been educated at Eton and Cambridge. He had carved out a career for himself as a photographer and earned respect as a man of independent mind.

He brought a new fresh style to the royal family. In the early years of marriage the Snowdons brought into their circle men and women who were creative in the worlds of the theatre, television and the arts generally.

Relations between East and West entered another bad period. When all was set for a summit meeting in Paris an American spy plane was shot down over Russia. Kruschev asked for an apology, almost as an ultimatum. President Eisenhower's visit to Moscow was called off. Kruschev went to address the United Nations in New York. His movements were restricted to Manhattan Island.

A Picasso exhibition at the Tate in London drew 450,000 visitors. It was boom-time for strip-clubs. There were estimated to be two hundred in London and another hundred in the provinces with one thousand girls performing the rites. *Lady Chatterley's Lover*, the sexually explicit classic by D. H. Lawrence, was published. There was a prosecution and an acquittal. The sales of the book were massive. There were new betting and gaming regulations permitting betting shops and casinos.

At the end of October the Queen and Prince Philip experienced a moment of danger. As they were coming back from a private visit to the King and Queen of Denmark their plane was on a collision course with two Sabre jets of the German air force. It was 'a near miss'.

In January 1961, the Queen and Prince Philip left for a two-month tour of India and Pakistan with short visits to Nepal, Persia and Turkey. On the way out she visited Cyprus and met Archbishop Makarios, president of the new republic of Cyprus, which had become a member of the Commonwealth.

India and Pakistan had joined the Commonwealth after their independence in 1947. It was still, however, remarkable that the Queen should be invited and greeted with such warmth after the long years of bitter struggle against British rule.

The two governments did their best to make it a pleasant as well as a political event. The Queen went to the races at Calcutta and Lahore. She walked with Prince Philip in the gardens of the Taj Mahal by moonlight. She stayed in the viceregal apartments in New Delhi, the vast administrative capital built by the British not many years before they left. In Pakistan she visited the Khyber Pass, the outpost of Empire where British and Indian troops had guarded the North-West Frontier.

Mr Nehru, the architect of the new India, was an urbane host. He was one of the most remarkable men of his generation, a complicated character compounded of the aristocratic Brahmin with the experience of Harrow and a number of British prisons in India.

A tiger shoot had been organized on an imperial scale with over two hundred beaters. The Queen was perched on a platform in one tree, Philip on another. He shot a tiger. A ceremonial picture was taken of the kill. The skin was to be made into a rug for Windsor Castle.

ABOVE The Missile Age. The Queen passes a Thunderbird during an inspection at Woolwich, the home of the Royal Artillery.

With Richard Nixon, then Vice-President in Eisenhower's administration, at the dedication of the America Memorial Chapel in St Paul's Cathedral, 1958.

ABOVE The opening of the St Lawrence Seaway in September 1959. With the Queen and Prince Philip are President Eisenhower and his wife and the Prime Minister of Canada, Mr John Diefenbaker and his wife.

LEFT Streamers in Bay Street during a drive through Toronto.

OPPOSITE ABOVE General de Gaulle comes to London in 1960 on a State Visit. He still said 'Non' to Britain joining the Common Market.

OPPOSITE BELOW A command performance at the Royal Opera House, Covent Garden. The visiting guests are the Shah of Iran and his Queen, who is on the right and wearing a tiara heavier than the Queen's. Later that year in 1959 the Shah divorced her and married his present Queen, Farah Diba.
Above the royal box are the peacock emblems of Iran.

TOP The 1962 Cup Final. Danny Blanchflower, captain of Tottenham Hotspur, is congratulated after beating Burnley 3–1. These were great days for Spurs. They had won the Cup the year before.

LEFT The royal train at Euston before the annual autumn trip to Balmoral. The corgis are familiar companions.

ABOVE Wimbledon 1960. It was the year Neale Fraser beat Rod Laver in the men's singles and Maria Bueno won the women's singles for the second time running.

Princess Margaret's 'lines'. Two queens and a prince as witnesses.

ABOVE Princess Margaret and Antony Armstrong-Jones leave for their honeymoon. A wave from her sister, the Queen. The Queen Mother looks happy. Starting with a cruise on the royal yacht *Britannia*, the couple had everything to look forward to.

The Visit to India – 1961

The President's reception at New Delhi. On the right is Mrs Pandit, sister of Mr Nehru, and herself an early High Commissioner for India in London. Sandhurst would have been proud of the officers in attendance.

Mr Nehru, creator of the new India, explains. A father of his country, a product of Harrow and British prisons in India.

The tiger Prince Philip shot as a guest of the Maharajah of Jaipur (standing next to the Queen).
The shot misfired. There was criticism in Britain where public opinion, as elsewhere, was concerned about the destruction of wildlife.

OPPOSITE Reflections at the Taj Mahal. The mausoleum outside Agra is of pure white marble. It was built by Shah Jehan in memory of his favourite wife, Mumtaz Mahal.

A tiger hunt in Nepal.

A regal entry into Jaipur.

But attitudes to killing rare wild beasts have changed in Britain and there was criticism in the press. Another tiger shoot had been arranged by King Mahendra of Nepal. Prince Philip developed a diplomatic whitlow on his trigger finger and left it to the royal staff to make the courtesy kills.

In London a serious crisis arose at a Commonwealth conference. South Africa found itself bitterly attacked for its apartheid policy (Sharpeville had become a symbol). On 15 March, Dr Verwoerd, the South African prime minister, announced that his country was leaving the Commonwealth.

The Queen and Prince Philip paid a state visit to Italy and met Pope John, who in a few years had won a world respect for the papacy such as it had not enjoyed for centuries. The Queen has never looked more splendid than she did at the audience. According to protocol, she was wearing black – a magnificent ankle-length laced gown, an elaborate veil thrown back to show her head, crowned with a superb tiara. The Italians, with their love of pageantry, gave her an enthusiastic welcome throughout the tour. She looked as if the Italian skies suited her very well.

Back in London the Queen met another remarkable man of God. Dr Billy Graham, the most compelling American evangelist of the post-war years, was invited with his wife to lunch at the Palace. He had for some years enjoyed a great reputation in Britain and his crusades here had a considerable impact at a time when such events seemed things of the past.

There was another royal wedding. The Duke of Kent married Katharine Worsley, daughter of one of the great Yorkshire magnates, in York Minster, which is in many ways to the north what Westminster Abbey is to the south. The choice of church was very popular in the area. Yorkshire is more a province than a county. It is as much a way of life as an area.

Two Russians and two Americans entered space – an awe-inspiring development at that time. The first man to circle the earth was a Russian, Major Gagarin. He came to London in July during the largest exhibition Russia had ever staged in a foreign country. Gagarin's modesty and charm made a great impression. The Queen invited him to lunch at the Palace. It was an agreeable gesture to Russian achievement.

Britain made an application to join the thriving Common Market. This was vetoed, after some discussion, by General de Gaulle.

Mr Macmillan reorganized his government. Mrs Margaret Thatcher appeared on the scene at the age of thirty-five in a junior position at the then Ministry of Pensions and National Insurance.

George Blake, one of most damaging Soviet spies, who had as a double agent caused irreparable damage and many deaths, was sentenced to forty-two years' imprisonment. His escape was organized soon after with an ease that infuriated the country. He found refuge and rewards in Russia.

A new world figure appeared – John Kennedy, the newly and narrowly elected President of the United States. Young, handsome, intelligent, articulate, he was determined to create a new image of the United States in its role as the richest and most powerful country in the world.

A Roman Catholic of Irish origin, he was a son of Joseph Kennedy who had acquired great wealth and influence with a ruthlessness that had made him unforgiving enemies. The new President had inherited many of them who considered that the White House had been bought for him, and that his overweening ambition and compulsive womanizing unfitted him for his office.

He came to Vienna to meet Mr Kruschev to discuss East–West relations. On his way back he had lunch with the Queen at the Palace. With him was his wife, Jacqueline, the cool, desirable sophisticate already embarked on her career of compulsive spending.

A new Archbishop of Canterbury was appointed. As head of the Anglican church the Queen takes a close interest in the major appointments. She is certainly consulted by the prime minister, who makes the decisions. Dr Fisher retired after reorganizing the church's finances to give every clergyman a reasonable living wage.

He had also played his part in the move towards reconciliation with the Roman Catholic Church and in 1960 had visited Pope John.

Dr Fisher's successor was Dr Ramsey, the Archbishop of York. A scholar and evangelist, he gave his support to the strengthening of links with Rome.

At the end of the year, the Queen, accompanied by Prince Philip, went to West Africa. She visited several countries including Ghana, a former colony, now a member of the Commonwealth. The country has great potential wealth and was led by one of the most dynamic new African leaders, Dr Nkrumah, who had also graduated from British prisons. He later fell from power, having acquired megalomaniac symptoms.

To finish the story of 1961 – the annual value of toys sold in Britain was £42m, compared with half a million pounds in 1938. That, even allowing for inflation, was a significant statistic.

In March 1962 Sir Martin Lindsay, a Conservative MP, tabled a motion attacking Lord Beaverbrook and his newspapers for running a 'sustained vendetta' against the royal family. It was Prince Philip who felt aggrieved and he said that he thought the *Daily Express* was 'bloody awful'.

There was criticism of the heavy cost of the government renovation of the apartments in Kensington Palace for Princess Margaret and Lord Snowdon.

Mr Macmillan's government was becoming unpopular in circles traditionally loyal to the Conservatives. Mr Selwyn Lloyd, the Chancellor of the Exchequer, produced a mainly neutral budget but imposed a levy on speculative gains.

This was bold, for it came after a statement by the then chairman of the Stock Exchange, Lord Ritchie of Dundee, 'I believe that the City has very nearly reached the end of its tether, and that its loyalty and willingness to co-operate have almost reached breaking point.'

Mr Macmillan, one of the shrewdest politicians of his age, knew affairs were not going well. In July he took drastic action. He sacked a third of his cabinet including Mr Selwyn Lloyd, his close friend Lord Kilmuir, the Lord Chancellor, and eight other ministers. Overnight the cartoonists abandoned 'Supermac' for 'Mac the Knife'.

He wrote in his diary: 'Well, it's all over. I am in bed, in mother's old bedroom, looking out into the garden and the woods.'

He wrote to the Queen: 'There are always ministers who are only making way to give place to younger men . . . but there are ministers who have ambition of higher things and who are rather badly wounded. All this, which involved I think twenty interviews in a space of about six hours, has left me very tired.'

The underlying problem was that Britain lacked a framework of economic planning such as its competitors in Europe had created after the war. Mr Macmillan and some of his colleagues recognized this. But it was not politic to put it squarely to the nation, so industry and the trade unions continued to operate in the blinkers of their short-term interests. Investment for the future was lagging; management was often ill-educated, and organized labour suspicious and unwilling to do more than negotiate current wage settlements.

In May the Queen was present with the Archbishops of Canterbury and York at the consecration of the new Coventry Cathedral, built alongside the ruins of the old which, with much of central Coventry, had been destroyed in one of the heaviest bombing raids of the war.

Britain's most prestigious artists had been employed to create a house of God, which would express the post-war age. Basil Spence was the architect. David Piper was responsible for the baptistery. Graham Sutherland designed the great tapestry of Christ in Glory which hangs behind the altar. The new cathedral was to become a focus of Christian activity for some of the most able of a new generation of clergy.

In June, the Queen's Gallery was opened in a specially constructed annexe of Buckingham Palace. There was a general feeling at the time that the public should have an opportunity of looking at some of the notable pictures from the royal collection, which is, as much by luck as judgment, remarkably rich.

The Royal Academy said that it was so hard-up that it would have to sell a famous heirloom, the Leonardo cartoon of *The Virgin and Child with St Anne and St John The Baptist*. The Academy demanded £800,000. The element of blackmail was apparent as there was a risk of a sale abroad. Finally, the money was raised – £450,000 from private sources and £350,000 from the state.

Final approval was given for a National Theatre on the South Bank, to be built with public money and supported by a subsidy. It had been a project ardently fought for over many years.

The Queen and Prince Philip, with outside advice, considered the choice of a school for Prince Charles who was nearly fourteen. He had been at a day school in Knightsbridge and then a boarder at Cheam, a preparatory school which Prince Philip had briefly attended.

Eton seemed the likely choice, but Philip had been at Gordonstoun in Scotland and wanted his son to follow him. He won the day.

The school was the creation of a German–Jewish educationalist, Dr Kurt Hahn. He had first established a school at Salem in South Germany after the First World War with the help of the last Imperial Chancellor, Prince Max of Baden, under whom Hahn had served.

Hahn, deeply influenced by Plato's *Republic* and the English public school system, wanted to create in Germany a school which would inculcate the best leadership qualities – moral and physical toughness, the desire to serve, the striving for excellence.

Hahn became a victim of the Nazis, but managed to reach Britain where, with the help of a group of aristocrats and academics who believed in his ideals, he re-created the school at Gordonstoun. Prince Philip, who had been at Salem, rejoined the school.

There was some doubt whether it was the right school for Charles. But, though he had initial difficulties, he did well.

Towards the end of October the end of the world was near for a large section of humanity. The United States came to the brink of an all-out nuclear war with Soviet Russia following the delivery to Cuba, then Soviet-dominated, of missiles which threatened large areas of the United States. President Kennedy decided on a show-down with Mr Kruschev.

Kennedy and his entourage, together with those chosen to survive a nuclear attack, were ready at the critical stage to move to their shelters. In other vulnerable countries such as Britain the number of adequate shelters was few and would have been enough for only a few leaders and essential survivors. The royal family had a high priority.

Finally, Kruschev, who had underestimated Kennedy when he met him at Vienna, climbed down and dismantled the Cuban missiles.

By 1963 a new generation of talented young men and women were finding a wide audience, especially on TV, with a form of satire which was a mixture of traditional undergraduate exuberance and a measure of social criticism. The BBC TV programme, 'That Was The Week That Was', gave it national significance.

The royal family was, like many other institutions, mocked, but compared with the savage attacks of the Regency and early Victoria era, quite gently. The satire, mild as it was, had its effect on the Queen who has a taste for mockery herself. She was thirty-seven and aware that a new generation was coming to the front with fresh attitudes. Some of the more pompous clichés certainly began to disappear from her speeches.

Princess Alexandra, daughter of the Duchess of Kent, married Angus Ogilvy, second son of the Earl of Airlie, in Westminster Abbey on 24 April. The Earl was very much of the court and had been Lord Chamberlain to the Queen Mother since 1937. Angus Ogilvy had gone into the City and acquired a large number of active directorships.

This year Mr Macmillan and his government were shaken by a sensational sex scandal which the press reported for months to an avid public. All other events faded into the background.

Mr Profumo, a government minister, resigned in the spring following the uncovering of an unsavoury world of prostitution and vice which he and other rich and influential people had frequented. In July Stephen Ward, an amiable, talented Bohemian, with wide social connections, who had drifted into the position of procurer, committed suicide at the end of his trial. . . . 'I'm sorry to disappoint the vultures.'

Christine Keeler, the most active and articulate call-girl in the case, became a national figure. The swimming-pool at Cliveden, where the Queen had attended the Daphne Fairbanks ball, became notorious as one of the meeting-places of the circle.

Even more seriously, British security was becoming a laughing-stock at home and abroad. In April, the findings of a judicial tribunal were published on the case of Vassall, an Admiralty clerk, who had been sentenced to eighteen years for espionage in Moscow and London. He was a vain young homosexual whose activities were for long unsuspected by British security.

In July the government admitted that 'Kim' Philby, one of the most senior men in British intelligence, had been during all his career a Soviet spy. This was after he had left Beirut for Moscow, to be followed shortly by his wife.

Britain's allies, especially the Americans, had good reason to doubt her trustworthiness if the intelligence and security services were so negligently run.

A well organized gang stole £2½m from a mail train in what has gone down in history as 'The Great Train Robbery'. Most of the gang were tracked down and given very long sentences. But spies who had caused many deaths and great damage to national security escaped immune, like Philby, or effected an easy escape from prison, like Blake.

Pope John died, mourned by the world. He had called together a Vatican Council charged to examine the Church and make such changes as were necessary for the future.

Hugh Gaitskell, leader of the Labour party, died untimely young. Brilliantly gifted, he had possessed the quality to lead Britain to a bright future when his party came to power. His mantle passed to Harold Wilson who defeated the other contender, George Brown, in the leadership election.

Dr Adenauer, who had survived the Hitler regime to lead post-war Western Germany, retired.

The Central African Federation, which had never had the stability hoped for, broke into three parts. Northern Rhodesia was to become independent as Zambia, Nyasaland as Malawi, but Southern Rhodesia, determined to retain white supremacy, decided to go it alone. It led to a break with Britain.

Mr Macmillan, dogged by many misfortunes this year, was finally struck down by an almost providential illness, resigned and with craft and skill organized the succession of Lord Home, the Foreign Secretary, as prime minister. Taking advantage of a new law, he disclaimed his peerage and entered the House of Commons as Sir Alec Douglas-Home. He was in all likelihood the last aristocrat to be prime minister.

Just after Mr Macmillan's resignation in October, the Queen wrote to him: 'For me it means that for the greater part of my reign you have not only been in charge of Britain's policies but you have been my guide and supporter through the mazes of international affairs and my instructor in many vital matters relating to our constitution and to the political and social life of my people.

'There is therefore no question of your successor, however admirable he may be, being able to perform exactly those services which you have given so generously and for which I am so deeply grateful.'

In November President Kennedy was assassinated in Dallas, Texas. He had recently returned from a triumphant tour of Western Europe during which, in the centre of Berlin only a stone's throw away from the Wall the Communists had built, he defiantly re-affirmed his resolution – 'Ich bin ein Berliner.'

His death was difficult to believe. He had embodied the vigour of life. With his vision of new frontiers for humanity he had given fresh hope not only to his country, but to the Western world which the United States led. His faults did not dim the light he gave and when it went out the world was a darker place.

The influences that caused his death are still mysterious. The assassination, five years later of his brother, Bobbie, already a contender for the presidency, threw more dark shadows on the American scene.

The sun no longer shone on Camelot, as the admirers had called the Kennedy court.

SEVEN

Swinging sixties

The Queen had her fourth child, Prince Edward, on 10 March 1964. There were reports in the foreign press that she was tired and depressed after the birth. It was said that she was even thinking of abdicating. The British press repeated these stories.

In the autumn the Queen appointed her first Labour prime minister, aged forty-eight, the youngest of the century. His party had won a narrow victory at the polls, ending a thirteen-year-rule by the Conservatives. Sir Alec Douglas-Home, the Conservative leader, had done much better than even his own party had expected.

The Labour government found itself faced with an immediate financial crisis. It had inherited a deficit of £750,000,000 and a fierce attack was launched on sterling by a group which became known as 'the Gnomes of Zurich'. They were to grow into ogres and remain as a nightmare for a long time.

A hard autumn budget was introduced. One of the emergency measures was a 15% surcharge on imports. The pound was salvaged with international help.

So Mr Wilson's government found itself hampered from the start from carrying out its programme of social reform.

Mr George Brown, second in power only to Mr Wilson, was put in charge of a new Department of Economic Affairs which was to plan economic strategy on a long-term basis beginning with a five year plan. The need for such measures had become increasingly clear to the more intelligent national leaders, irrespective of party.

But the innovation came to naught, in spite of the enthusiasm of Mr Brown and the small group of civil servants and outside advisers he recruited.

It encountered the implacable hostility of the Treasury which saw the new

46

department as a challenge to its previously undisputed power. Mr James Callaghan, then Chancellor of the Exchequer, was in charge of the Treasury.

In the United States President Johnson, who being Vice-President had gone to the White House on the murder of Kennedy, was now elected president by a large majority. A shrewd, earthy, brilliantly successful politician, he was to put through more liberal measures, especially in the field of civil rights, than anyone thought possible. Kennedy was dead, but Johnson made his ideals reality.

Unfortunately, he inherited more than liberal ideals from Kennedy. He inherited a growing involvement in Vietnam.

Mr Nehru died. Mr Kruschev, who had led Soviet Russia out of the Stalin era, was deposed. Unlike former Soviet leaders, he was allowed to live out his life in comfortable retirement. China exploded its first atom bomb.

Mr Wilson discussed with the Queen the fundamental changes he was going to make in the awarding of honours. He would recommend no more hereditary titles and would introduce a new citation, 'for services to export'. In the first honours list he submitted to the Queen at the end of the year there were many more industrialists and more names from the worlds of sport, entertainment and the arts. Stanley Matthews, the footballer, was made a Knight. Ena Sharples of the TV series, *Coronation Street*, was given an MBE.

The Beatles, who were at the height of their astonishing world reputation, were awarded MBEs. This caused controversy and some former recipients returned their decorations.

But the honours list was less stuffy and orthodox, which was Mr Wilson's intention.

On 24 January 1965, Sir Winston Churchill died, full of years and fame. The nation, the Commonwealth, the world mourned him. Three hundred thousand people filed through Westminster Hall where he lay in state. Parliament was adjourned until the funeral, which he had partly organized himself. Twenty-five million people in Britain, half the population, watched the ceremony on television.

It was a sombrely magnificent occasion with all the military pomp that Churchill desired. The Queen, who according to a curious rule of protocol only attends the funerals of her family, led the mourning. It would have been unthinkable for her not to be there.

Mr Wilson recalls in his memoirs a curious incident about Ian Smith at the Churchill funeral. The Rhodesian leader was in London and although relations were already very difficult, there were still many links with Britain. Mr Wilson asked the Queen if Mr Smith could be invited to the Palace reception for the world leaders who had come for the funeral. She agreed and an invitation was sent.

When the reception had been going on for some time the Queen noticed that Mr Smith was not there. She asked Mr Wilson what had happened to him. He said he did not know.

An equerry was sent to find him and found him eating a steak in the restaurant of the Hyde Park Hotel. He said he had never received the invitation and back at the Palace stammered out his excuses to the Queen.

Mr Wilson says that he was told later on good authority the invitation was in his pocket all the time.

Financially, the year was another difficult one with sterling under continual pressure. The City was bitter about the Government's Capital Gains and Corporation Taxes. An added source of bitterness in the managerial class was the taxing of expense accounts unless they involved exports. The free-spending atmosphere disappeared from bars, restaurants and hotels.

A conflict broke out between India and Pakistan. It was not extensive nor protracted, but it left bitterness between the two Commonwealth countries.

The Conservative MPs changed their leader. Sir Alec Douglas-Home, who had only narrowly lost the election the previous year, was replaced by Mr Edward Heath. The Conservatives had decided to change their image. The aristocrat was set aside for a man who had made his way in life from a lower middle-class background. He had won a scholarship to Oxford, had commanded an artillery battery in the war and then devoted himself to politics. He had proved in office a first-class organizer as Chief Whip. He was a bachelor, made his own decisions and was dedicated to British membership of the Common Market. He provided edge and energy as Opposition Leader.

The Queen and Prince Philip visited West Germany. He had gone there often to see his sisters who had married Germans. But for Elizabeth it was a first visit.

The Germans were proud to show her the impressive record of their energy, including the cities that had been rebuilt from the rubble of 1945.

But the hosts also gave her an opportunity of seeing some of the beauty of their country. They stayed in the famous Hotel Petersberg, high on a hill looking down over the Rhine landscape. They travelled south past romantic castles with old villages grouped around the walls. In the rolling wooded country that slopes down to Lake Constance, they visited Salem where Prince Philip had first been taught by Kurt Hahn.

The Queen was able to see something of the Germany of scholarship, music and kindliness that the evil years had almost extinguished.

The Queen met many of the princely families to whom she is related and pleased them with an encyclopaedic knowledge of the genealogical trees.

Prince Charles was finishing at Gordonstoun this year and his parents went to see the production of *Macbeth*, which is something of a school ritual. Prince Philip had had a role in his days there and now Prince Charles also played a part in the blood-stained story in which some of his ancestors appear.

He was soon leaving for Australia to spend a term or two at Geelong, which is run on English public school lines with a strong accent on out-of-door activities.

Southern Rhodesia in a Unilateral Declaration of Independence (UDI) broke away from Britain to pursue under its leader, Mr Ian Smith, a policy of white supremacy. The Organization of African Unity (OAU) was growing in strength as the continent became increasingly free.

Mr Wilson called a spring election in 1966 and Labour was returned with a comfortable majority. On 16 May a seamen's strike was called and proved the most damaging industrial dispute since the war. A State of Emergency was declared on 23 May. Mr Wilson named eight communists who occupied strategic posts in the union. The strike continued for forty-seven days until 1 July. It increased international concern for the state of Britain.

The World Cup soccer finals were held in Britain. The BBC televised the matches nearly every evening for almost three weeks. Millions who had never seen a soccer match became enthusiasts. To crown it all England won the final at Wembley. The Queen was at the game. By means of Eurovision and the communications satellite, Telstar, the world watched the match. It was estimated that several hundred millions saw the game.

There was good news from the North Sea. Natural gas had been found in the British sector and it could now be said with confidence that there was enough for most of Britain's needs for a considerable number of years. Exploration for oil was beginning further north. The experts were cautiously hopeful.

In October a slag-heap fell on a school at Aberfan, a mining village in South Wales. The 144 victims were mainly children. Prince Philip went to the scene while rescue operations were being mounted. The appeal that followed had a response that was a national tribute to the mining community. From abroad help poured in.

Mr Wilson announced there would be no more honours given to political party workers and officials. He said that in the post-war years these awards had become a form of political patronage and that in the future it would be public service which would be recognized, irrespective of party.

Sanctions had been imposed on Rhodesia, now in rebellion against Britain. There was a great deal of sympathy for the white Rhodesians. They tended to come from ordinary families and had by hard work and initiative created their own prosperity. During the war their young men had cheerfully enlisted to help fight Britain's war. Ian Smith joined the RAF and became a fighter pilot. He was shot down twice. After the first crash he had plastic surgery. The second time he came down in Italy behind the German lines and joined the partisans. It was difficult to consider these men, so patriotic and loyal to the Crown, as disloyal or rebels.

At the beginning of December Mr Wilson had a meeting with Mr Smith in the cruiser, HMS *Tiger* at Gibraltar. But the talks led nowhere.

EIGHT

Strife and success

In February 1967 the Queen gave a state banquet at Buckingham Palace for Mr Kosygin, who had succeeded Mr Kruschev as Leader of Soviet Russia. As a gesture, evening dress was not worn. It was meant well. But in Republican France Soviet guests invited to state banquets comply with the rule of formal dress.

Mr Kosygin, a man of craggy looks and personal charm, had a successful tour of England and Scotland. He told the Queen she would be a welcome guest in his country.

Mr Wilson tried hard during the visit to act as an intermediary in a settlement of the Vietnam war, now of appalling dimensions. But his efforts ended in failure. Probably the Americans no longer considered Britain to rank the role of peacemaker.

Canada was celebrating the centenary of its Dominion status with a stupendous exhibition, 'Expo '67'. The Queen went with Prince Philip, who returned twice more. Other members of the family went in force.

In June the Queen unveiled a plaque in London on the hundredth anniversary of the birth of her grandmother, Queen Mary. The Duke of Windsor, who was her eldest son, was asked over from France with his wife for the ceremony. It was the first time the Queen had met the Duchess, who had been married to her uncle for thirty years.

The Earl of Harewood, a cousin of the Queen, was divorced by his wife for adultery. He already had a child by the woman in question and wished to marry her. First he had to obtain the Queen's consent 'on the advice of the Cabinet'. This was necessary under the Royal Marriages Act of 1772, a measure introduced by George III to stop his children making marriages he did not approve of. Its use in 1967 seemed quaint.

In a six-day campaign beginning on 5 June, Israel in a surprise attack routed the forces of Egypt and Jordan. The gains were Jerusalem and the

Sinai right up to the banks of the Suez Canal. It was a great military achievement. But the fruits of victory were to turn sour later.

The Arab countries were learning to co-operate and use the weapon of oil supplies with devastating effect. The Suez Canal was closed. An embargo was placed on oil exports, which, fortunately for the industrialized countries, did not last long. But the message was clear.

A serious internal conflict started in Nigeria, later called the Biafran civil war. It was a setback for this powerful country, about to enjoy increased prosperity and power as an oil exporter.

It was a shrewd move this year to invite King Faisal of Saudi Arabia, the richest oil country of all, to London for a state visit to the Queen. She also went to France to look at some of the renowned studs there. She stayed at a splendid ducal chateau and had a good time. It may be that the visit was designed to help the second application to join the Common Market. If so, it was in vain. De Gaulle vetoed it.

In July the Queen went down to Greenwich and knighted Francis Chichester, the veteran sailor who had completed a round-the-world single-handed journey in his yacht. She dubbed him on the same spot where Queen Elizabeth I had knighted Francis Drake on his return from his profitable circumnavigation of the world in which she had a financial interest. This was a happy occasion. But there was a sad irony in the comparison between the man who opened up the oceans to our commerce and an intrepid amateur yachtsman.

The breathalyser, testing the amount of alcohol consumed by a motorist, was introduced and has saved many lives. An act was passed to help tackle the growing problem of drug-taking, especially among the young.

In November the City was swept by rumours of a sterling devaluation. The mood grew to one of panic. On the eighteenth it happened. Sterling was devalued by 14·3%. Mr Wilson and his Chancellor, Mr Callaghan, had battled for three years to preserve the value of the pound. It was seen as a serious set-back and a blow to national pride, for the days of floating currencies had not yet arrived.

The consequences of the devaluation became clear in 1968 – rising prices, more taxation, cuts in government expenditure which included defence economies and a withdrawal of the British presence east of Suez, a recognition that in military terms Britain was no longer a world power. (The Conservatives later sent back token forces east.)

In March Mr George Brown resigned as Foreign Secretary and deputy prime minister. He had great qualities, including a measure of vision, increasingly rare among politicians. But other aspects of his character had severely tried his colleagues.

A Race Relations Board was set up to deal with racial discrimination. It was a time when Asians were flooding in from East Africa where the new black governments were expelling them. This was the time when Mr Enoch Powell, the brilliant Conservative politician, exacerbated the situation with his rhetoric: 'As I look ahead, I am filled with foreboding. Like the Roman I seem to see the River Tiber foaming with blood.' The Conservative opposition leaders disowned him, but his words found a wide response which cut across party. His mail, acclaiming him, was numbered in tens of thousands. In the country there was an almost reverential support for him among the Conservative rank-and-file, who saw him as a national saviour and found Edward Heath uninspiring.

London Bridge, which was being replaced, was sold for two and a half million dollars to an American company and transferred to Lake Havasu City on the River Colorado as a tourist attraction. It was not exactly an historic monument. It was only 136 years old.

The age of majority was reduced from twenty-one to eighteen, to be followed by the vote at the same age. The Pope came out against contraception and created dissension, especially among Catholic women. In May a wave of unrest broke out in Paris and the provinces. Students and workers manned the barricades and occupied factories and universities. De Gaulle rode out the storm – but the writing was on the wall.

In the Middle East the Arabs were organizing guerrilla groups against Israel. The Palestinian Liberation Organisation (PLO) was becoming a force to reckon with.

Princess Margaret inaugurated a hovercraft service between Dover and Boulogne. The craft travelled at seventy-five mph and could carry 254 passengers and thirty vehicles. It was a triumph for British technology.

In August Russian tanks moved into Czechoslovakia and crushed the Dubcek government which had shown signs of establishing a more liberal regime.

The Queen and her family were heavily involved this year and until May 1969 in the filming of 'Royal Family' for television. It was a joint BBC–ITV production. According to Andrew Duncan in *The Reality of Monarchy*, the production team spent seventy-five days in 172 locations. 'Forty-three hours of film had to be cut into what was anticipated as an hour but was extended to 110 minutes in England.'

The Queen had had some misgivings about 'over-exposure'. But the film did its job well. It showed, inevitably in a flattering light, aspects of the life of the family as they went about their duties or relaxed. The film had great success in Britain, the Commonwealth, the United States and elsewhere.

In the United States the Americans, including President Johnson, were realizing that the Vietnam war was both unjust and unwinnable. Student demonstrations, sometimes ending in deaths, swept not only the United States, but spread throughout the world. The students' idealism was used by communist and anarchist bodies to foment trouble. In London there was a great 'demo' in October ending in Grosvenor Square, alongside the American Embassy. Hard-line trouble-makers must have wept to learn that it broke up during the night with the police and remaining demonstrators singing 'Auld Lang Syne'. At the end of the year Nixon was elected President by a small majority. His first task was to extricate the Americans from Vietnam – whatever the cost in national pride.

Oil was being discovered in large quantities off the coast of Scotland by British, American and other oil companies. The Scottish Nationalists, up to now a fringe party, began to grow in strength as the promise of oil revenues grew in Scottish minds.

Mr Wilson had another fruitless meeting with Mr Ian Smith of Rhodesia in another British warship at Gibraltar.

Towards the end of the year the world financial markets were moving towards chaos. Even the dollar was under attack. De Gaulle was thought to be behind this.

There were heavy sales of sterling and a mood of panic gripped the City of London. In one day in December there were rumours that Mr Wilson was going to resign, that there was to be a coalition government and that the Queen was abdicating.

In January 1969 there was a Commonwealth Prime Ministers' conference in London attended by twenty-eight nations. There were differences of opinion and Britain was having to learn that it was no longer the boss. *The Daily Telegraph* said that the Commonwealth had become a harmful nuisance and that Britain should withdraw.

A man who made considerable impact was Pierre Trudeau, the handsome young prime minister of Canada. He was brilliant, full of ideas and his French-Canadian background influenced his views at this time. 'The values of the new generation and tremendous technological changes may lead Canada to give up its connections with the royal family in the next decade.'

In February Mr Nixon came to London with his wife and was entertained

Eton. After morning service in the chapel, the Queen walks through School Yard. Eton was not to be Prince Charles's school, as had been expected. He went to Gordonstoun.

Kilts at Balmoral. With the Queen is her late uncle, the Duke of Gloucester. A Scottish regiment always provides the guard at Balmoral.

LEFT On the Shetland Islands. Inspecting livestock at Fraser Park, Scalloway.

BELOW Handicapped scouts at the St George's Day Parade of Queen's Scouts at Windsor Castle. With the Queen is the Chief Scout, Lord Maclean, who since 1971 has been her Lord Chamberlain.

OPPOSITE After the consecration of the new Coventry Cathedral, built alongside the ruins of the old, destroyed with much of the centre of the city in one of the heaviest air-raids of the war. The bronze group by Epstein shows St Michael overcoming the devil.

OPPOSITE ABOVE Waiting for the bride, 1963. But Princess Alexandra did arrive to marry Angus Ogilvy.

OPPOSITE BELOW A look of incredulity for Sir Robert Menzies, Prime Minister of Australia.

ABOVE There were 1000 aborigines to see the Queen at Alice Springs in the Australian Northern Territory.
The town had a population of only 5000, but Nevil Shute's book, *A Town Like Alice*, had made it world-famous.

RIGHT Charlottetown, capital of Prince Edward Island, Canada. Leaving the royal yacht for a performance at the Memorial Theatre.

ABOVE Polo at Windsor, 1964. Something amusing in the programme. Lord Mountbatten smiles, but Prince Charles keeps his head down.

RIGHT A gift from Canada. Mr Lester Pearson, the Prime Minister, shows off the mini-car and trailer.

BELOW A gathering of the tribesmen at El Obeid in the Sudan, which had become an independent state.

OPPOSITE ABOVE The State Visit to West Germany in 1965. It was twenty years after the end of the war. Now Germany was an ally, rich and powerful.

OPPOSITE BELOW The village of Salem in Southern Germany. Prince Philip wanted to show the Queen the former monastery where he had gone to school under Dr Kurt Hahn before he left Nazi Germany and started up again at Gordonstoun.

ABOVE Jacqueline Kennedy with her son John follows the Queen at the unveiling of a memorial to her husband, President Kennedy, at Runnymede, where King John granted the Magna Carta. 'With all our hearts,' the Queen said at the ceremony, 'my people shared his triumphs, grieved at his reverses, and wept at his death.'

RIGHT A changing Britain. The Queen sees fresh faces at an art class.

by the Queen. He gave the impression of a strong, forceful personality determined to break down barriers which were shutting the world into two armed camps.

In March Concorde, the Anglo–French supersonic passenger aircraft, made its maiden flight at Toulouse. The costs of the project were mounting to a frightening level.

Eisenhower died and the leaders of the world were at his funeral. The Queen was represented by Lord Mountbatten. There was criticism that the Queen had not gone. Eisenhower had played a great part as a war leader in the West and was popular here. But the protocol that the Queen attends the funerals only of her family held fast. The only exception had been for Churchill.

The violence in Ulster, long simmering, erupted and British troops were involved in trying to keep a semblance of order as the Protestant majority and the Catholic minority tore the province to pieces. It was the beginning of another long chapter in blood-stained history of relations between Britain and Ireland. It was to test the patience of politicians of both parties in Westminster. It was to test the patience of the British when the IRA brought their bombs and guns to London and other cities.

In France de Gaulle was defeated in an election and nursed his wounded pride for a time in Ireland from which some of his ancestors had come. In Germany Willy Brandt was elected Chancellor, a milestone in the history of his country and of Europe. An active resister to Nazi Germany, he had become Mayor of Berlin and stood firm when the Russians built their Wall. He represented the liberal traditions of Germany, so long submerged.

On 1 July, Prince Charles was invested as Prince of Wales at Caernarvon Castle. He had by now taken a degree in archaeology and anthropology at Cambridge, learned some Welsh at the University College of Wales at Aberystwyth and pursued his naval career.

Before the investiture there were criticisms that the ceremony was a costly anachronism and would be mocked by the young. It was pointed out that groups of extreme Welsh were planting bombs and security would be difficult.

But it turned out a great success. The event, organized by the Duke of Norfolk and Lord Snowdon, was dominated by the TV technicians, now filming in colour. There were around four to five thousand at the Castle, but the world-wide TV audience was counted in hundreds of millions.

On his twenty-first birthday in November Prince Charles had a great party with over four hundred guests with all the appropriate jollification, including fireworks. He also had invited Yehudi Menuhin to take an orchestra to the Palace – a gesture that was noted.

These events produced another crop of rumours that the Queen would be abdicating. This time they were based on the fact that if his mother lived a normal life span, Charles would be an old man before he came to the throne.

At this time, his father, Prince Philip had informed the American public in a TV programme that the royal family was 'going into the red'. He added, 'If nothing happens we shall have to – I don't know, we may have to move into smaller premises, who knows? . . . We've closed down – well, for instance, we had a small yacht which we've had to sell, and I shall probably have to give up polo fairly soon, things like that.'

His remarks caused an uproar back in Britain. Mr Wilson said in Parliament that talks about the royal finances had been going on for some time between the Treasury and Palace officials. He said that his government had told the Palace that the matter would be dealt with by the next Government – an election was not far off. He added that there was adequate machinery to deal with any emergencies for the time being.

The royal family, like the Queen's subjects, like the world in general, was feeling the impact of inflation.

Mr Wilson had greater problems than polo to worry about. His attempt to modify the negotiating freedom of the trade unions, the policy called 'In Place of Strife' and introduced by Mrs Barbara Castle, one of the most trusted of his ministers, had to be withdrawn in face of resolute opposition by the trade unions.

It was a major defeat for a Labour government.

The trade unions' freedoms remained untouched. The question was – for how long?

The American space programme, launched by President Kennedy, achieved miraculous successes that year. On 21 July man set foot on the moon and the world saw it by television. The landing from *Apollo 12* in November was even more spectacular. But the costs were astronomical and taxing even American resources.

NINE

End of an epoch

1970

At the beginning of 1970 it became known that Mrs Muriel McKay, wife of the deputy chairman of the *News of the World*, had been kidnapped and that a ransom of one million pounds was being demanded. The first of the new-style kidnappings, already prevalent in the United States and Italy, had happened in Britain. Her body was never found. Two West Indian brothers were found guilty and sent to prison for life.

In January the Biafran civil war came to an end. The Nigerian administration, headed by General Gowan, proved magnanimous in victory and set about restoring peace and prosperity.

That winter, a young South African, Peter Hain, who had achieved a national position as leader of the Young Liberals and organizer of anti-apartheid demonstrations, mounted a campaign against the South African rugby team, the Springboks, which was touring Britain. It caused trouble, but did not stop the matches.

Success was achieved, however, in stopping the tour of the South African cricket team which was due in the summer. It became clear the matches would have to be played behind barbed wire and with massive police protection. Finally, Mr Callaghan, the Home Secretary, with Mr Wilson's agreement, asked the MCC to call off the tour, which it did 'with regret'.

Mr Ian Smith declared Rhodesia an independent republic at the beginning of March. To the Rhodesians' discomfiture, most countries, including the United States, withdrew their diplomats.

The Queen spent nearly two months away in the spring with her husband, Charles and Anne, on a tour of Australia, New Zealand and the South Seas. There was greater informality in the arrangements and the Queen looked relaxed as she mingled with the crowds. It was not an easy accomplishment.

A general election was in the offing and after years when the opinion polls had pronounced that Mr Wilson and his government were unpopular, they announced there was a switch towards them. But strike still followed strike. Mr Wilson's attempts to obtain either a voluntary or compulsory wages policy had failed, as had the measures to control prices.

When the election came in June a newspaper strike stopped the press. Mr Wilson intervened personally to settle it as he wished to ensure that the flow of news and comment could be restored at such a vital time for a democracy.

Mr Heath led the Conservatives to victory, in spite of the opinion polls and the faint-hearts in his own party. The victory was very much his. It gave him a personal authority that he showed he would use.

He said at the Conservative victory conference in October: 'We were returned to office to change the course and the history of this nation, nothing else. And it is this new course which the government is now shaping.'

Above all, he saw his mission as the entry of Britain into the Common Market. With de Gaulle out of the way, he saw no insuperable obstacle. He appointed his closest confidant, Mr Anthony (later Lord) Barber, to lead the negotiations.

In the January before the election, Mr Heath had held a policy conference at the Selsdon Park Hotel, Croydon. There was born the image of what was mockingly called, 'Selsdon Man'.

The policy agreed was to reduce the level of direct taxation; to impose immigration controls; to curb strikes by making agreements between employers and unions enforceable at law. There was also an underlying theme which reflected grass-roots Conservative thinking. There was to be more discipline in life. The slogan was, 'Law and Order'.

But it is now acknowledged that Edward Heath won the election in its last week by more mundane methods. He, the bachelor, won over the house-wives by attacking the rise in prices in the shops and promising to do something about it.

Mr Iain Macleod, the new Chancellor of the Exchequer, died a few weeks after taking office. It was a loss not only to the government, but to his party and the country. For he represented with brilliance a liberal capitalism, conscious of social justice, that had found a response in many hearts as well as minds. His loss was later seen to be irreparable, just as was the earlier loss to Labour of Hugh Gaitskell. They both stood head and shoulders above their peers.

Macleod was succeeded by Anthony Barber, who had scarcely had time to open his Common Market brief. He had already considerable experience as a Treasury minister.

After a trip to Canada with their parents, Charles and Anne in July were for a few days guests of President Nixon and his wife. It was not a happy event for Anne. She showed she resented the uninhibited approach of the American journalists and, in consequence, got a bad press.

In July two gas bombs were thrown from a public gallery into the House of Commons. It was a protest against their use in Ulster. The event led to a hurried review of security, not only at Westminster. Suddenly Britain realized how vulnerable its open way of life was. Since then, due to threats and outrages, measures have had to be taken to try and safeguard government offices, national galleries and museums, foreign embassies, transport, theatres, restaurants and public houses. It is an extra burden on the police, but the necessary measures have been accepted by the public with traditional phlegm.

This was all part of a new wave of terrorism that was sweeping the world. In September there was an extraordinary series of aircraft hijackings by Palestinian Arab organizations. Miss Leila Khaled, a young terrorist, was captured after attempting with others to take over an Israeli airliner which had left London for America. She was brought back to Britain and kept in custody, but the lives of over two hundred innocent passengers held hostage at the same time on a Jordanian airstrip were at stake. The blackmail succeeded. Miss Khaled was flown out in an RAF plane to Cairo, collecting six other Arab prisoners en route.

Mr Barber brought in an autumn budget with measures which delighted the Conservatives. There were major cuts in taxation met in part by increased charges for some social services and cuts in others. As a result there were increases in the cost of food, rents for council tenants and commuters' fares in the London area. There was, however, a provision to ensure a guaranteed minimum wage for the first time.

The Conservatives tasted these first fruits of victory and found them palatable. It was a budget in favour of the middle classes.

There was one curious pinch-penny measure, more dear to Mr Heath than Mr Barber. Charges were imposed for admission to the national art galleries and museums. Mr Heath's interest in music had led people to think he was a man of culture and there was surprise at the measure. It grew to an uproar, even among traditional Conservative supporters, when it was realized that the cost of collecting the money would equal the charges and that legal trusts would have to be broken.

Mr Heath remained adamant. He believes there is a price for all pleasures. It was not a storm in a tea-cup. It was enlightening.

The charges were finally imposed not long before Mr Heath lost power. They were quietly withdrawn by the new Labour government.

A new star in the Conservative government was Mr John Davies, former head of the CBI, who was appointed Minister of Technology. 'Lame ducks' were his bane. 'I will not,' he said firmly, 'bolster up or bail out companies where I can see no end to the process of propping them up.'

He was soon faced with a case in point. In November, Rolls-Royce, a company in which the country took pride and which the world acknowledged as a symbol of British quality, ran into serious financial difficulties. It was first propped up and then, in the early months of 1971, became bankrupt and had to be nationalized by the Conservative government.

The root of the trouble was a foolish open-ended contract for the supply of the RB 211-22 engine for the American Lockheed TriStar jet.

Rolls-Royce had to be saved. It was a major employer. It was one of the world's leading manufacturers of aircraft engines. It was a major earner of foreign currency.

The Rolls-Royce car division was not affected by the crisis. For the Queen, however, the RR troubles had a close interest. For she, more than most of her subjects, is accustomed to the superb engineering and elegant luxury of the cars. She has a fleet of them.

The Conservatives had committed themselves before the election to the supply of arms to South Africa. Britain had banned them for some time as a gesture against apartheid. But the Conservatives said that the arms were needed, not for suppressing the black population, but to defend sea-routes vital for Britain, NATO and the free world.

Mr Heath's government set about keeping their pledge. As a result before the end of the year the Commonwealth was in danger of dissolving. Nigeria said, 'Whether or not the Commonwealth continues will be, to our mind, the responsibility of Britain.' Tanzania and Zambia told Mr Heath bluntly of their similar attitude.

The danger was that Mr Heath had never cared greatly for the Commonwealth. His eyes were fixed on one goal . . . Europe.

However, he, and his Foreign Secretary, Sir Alec Douglas-Home, were disturbed to learn that in the United States Mr Nixon's administration would not support their South Africa arms policy. Nor would Mr Trudeau of Canada.

In taking notes of these developments, the Queen was also aware of the attitude of the Anglican Church of which she is the head. The Archbishop of Canterbury, supported by a hundred Anglican bishops of many countries, came out with a strong condemnation of South Africa.

On 3 December the government published its Industrial Relations Bill, which proposed to set up a National Industrial Relations Court with the status of a High Court and enabled to make collective agreements reached between unions and employers enforceable at law.

This was at a time of considerable industrial unrest and many strikes. The electricity power workers started a work to rule which was devastatingly effective. On 12 December the Queen signed the proclamation of a state of emergency.

She also had to have tea by candlelight in Buckingham Palace.

The work to rule was called off two days later and the dispute referred to a court of enquiry. There were lights enough for the Christmas celebrations.

Selsdon Man had been in power for less than six months.

In Glasgow at the beginning of 1971 there was an appalling accident at the end of a football match at Ibrox Park between Glasgow Rangers and Celtic. In a stampede sixty-six were killed and 145 injured.

The home of the Minister of Employment, Mr Robert (later Lord) Carr was bombed. Fortunately, the family was away.

Decimalization Day came for Britain on 15 February 1971, with its organizers addressing the public with naïve advice in a mood of self-congratulation. Accepting that decimalization was necessary – it was not a party matter – the commission had produced a method of such appalling stupidity that in a more just society its members would have been impeached. It is generally recognized that their efforts contributed largely to the rate of inflation.

Mr Barber had a worrying year at the Treasury. Unemployment was rising and reached nearly a million – a figure that was considered at that time socially unacceptable and politically damaging. There were increases in old age pensions and other welfare payments. There were various reflationary measures to boost the economy. But they did not work.

With rising unemployment and the setting up of the Industrial Relations Court, the mood of the unions was hardening. Strikes were becoming bitter.

Sir Alec Douglas-Home, the Foreign Secretary, expelled a hundred Russians who had under one guise or another enjoyed diplomatic status in London. At one stroke it put an end to an intolerable situation.

Mr Heath returned unhappy from a Commonwealth Prime Ministers' Conference in Singapore. He said much of the old intimacy had gone. He found it difficult to appreciate that Britain could no longer dominate the Commonwealth. His mood made him all the more determined to press on with the Common Market negotiations with missionary zeal.

Malta, where the Queen had spent happy days in the early years of her marriage, was becoming a costly embarrassment to Britain. Mr Mintoff, the able and aggressive leader of the island, obtained large grants from Britain, but they were never enough. He banked on gratitude for the fortitude of the Maltese during the war and the British need of the island as a naval base. But gratitude was fading and the base becoming increasingly less important as the Mediterranean fleet shrunk.

As Minister of Education and Science, Mrs Margaret Thatcher was making her mark. Her administrative skills developed and she showed a nineteenth-century belief in self-reliance, a relentless competitive drive and urge to succeed.

The ten-year census showed that the population of Britain had increased by 2,600,000 to 48,815,000.

Near Baker Street, London, the home of Sherlock Holmes (one cannot say, mythical), a gang broke into the vaults of a bank and plundered many strong-boxes. It was a great haul, but its extent will never be known for they contained much undeclared wealth. All the impedimenta of modern technology were used, including walkie-talkies.

In September the Queen had the pleasure of presenting her daughter, Anne, with a gold medal, trophy and £250 for winning the individual European championship at the Burghley horse trials. Anne's devotion to a highly competitive sport, not without physical danger, showed her mettle.

The Queen had a difficult state visit in October. She received the Emperor and Empress of Japan. For reasons of state it was a necessary visit. Japan has become an economic giant whose people has dedicated itself since its defeat to production with the same fervour it gave to war.

The barbarities of the Japanese towards prisoners-of-war were not forgotten, nor forgiven. Lord Mountbatten, who had commanded in the Far East, refused to attend the welcoming ceremonies, but at the Queen's entreaty, relented and had a short audience of the Emperor.

The British showed their attitude in the streets by their absence.

The terms obtained for joining the Common Market were debated in the House of Commons at the end of October. In an open vote, which split party loyalties, approval was given by the handsome majority of 112. It was a triumph for Mr Heath. 'We have the chance of new greatness,' he said at this time. 'Now we must take it.'

At the end of the year the royal finances came up for review. It was not a good time. Prices were rising considerably; unemployment was higher than it had been for many years; nearly all income groups were thinking in terms of cutting back expenditure. But then it is never a good time to ask for more money. Both inside and outside the House of Commons it was generally appreciated that to keep up standards at home and abroad the royal family needed an increase.

A select committee sat for some months and heard evidence from Palace officials and others. The whole business of royal finances is infinitely complicated and surrounded by a lot of mumbo-jumbo. What became clear was that the Queen had no intention of disclosing the extent of the royal personal fortune which has been built up since the time of the frugal Prince Albert with the help of tax concessions, exemption from death duties and astute management. Wild estimates of its extent have been made. It may well be of the order of £15–20 millions.

The committee reported to the House suggesting that the £475,000 annual payments of the Civil List should be increased to £980,000.

This was agreed. But there was criticism from quarters normally well-disposed. There was the question of tax concessions given on the payments made to members of the royal family. There was a feeling that the business of providing for the royal family should be rationalized. Mr Douglas Houghton, a distinguished chairman of the Parliamentary Labour Party, suggested to the select committee that the royal household should be reconstituted as a department of state under the control of a new body, 'the Commissioners of the Crown'. The proposal was rejected by only one vote.

More finance was found for Concorde, but politicians and public alike were wondering just how much the project was going to cost. Many experts were saying with increasing cogency that the basic concept was wrong.

Another immigration problem was causing general concern. The Kenyan Asians were being hounded out and as many had British passports, they had the right of entry.

China began to lift what had been called the bamboo curtain. Beginning with table-tennis competitions, relations with the outside world were quietly established as China realized its isolation at a time when its fear of Russia was growing.

Sir Alec Douglas-Home had hoped to find a settlement of the Rhodesian problem which had eluded Mr Wilson. But he found Ian Smith unbending and sanctions imposed earlier were renewed. It was a disappointment for Sir Alec. Among Conservatives even, patience with the Rhodesians from now on waned.

On 22 January 1972 Mr Heath signed the Treaty of Accession to the Common Market in Brussels. There followed many weeks of acrimonious debate in the House of Commons on the necessary legislation. It cut across party loyalties. There were those who feared the inevitable loss of sovereignty; there were those who feared the effect on Commonwealth links; there were those who thought the terms negotiated by the Government were onerous and ill-considered; there were those who thought the British people were being bulldozed into a decision that would fundamentally change their way of life. Finally, the measures were passed 309–301, a very narrow margin.

In February the Queen and Prince Philip, accompanied by Anne, went on an extended tour of the East – Thailand, Malaysia, Singapore, Brunei, Malacca, the Seychelles, Mauritius. An important visit was made to Kenya where they had lunch with President Kenyatta in Nairobi. He was leading his country into the future with skill and determination.

In Britain the new Industrial Relations Court, presided over by its high court judge, Sir John Donaldson, found itself almost immediately presented with Trade Union defiance. Fines were imposed, unpaid and followed by greater fines. Five dockers were sent to gaol for contempt of court. Donaldson said: 'By their conduct these men are saying they are above the rule of law. No court should ignore such a challenge. To do so would imperil all law and order.'

As a judge administering the law, he was right. But the situation was fraught with political and economic dangers that were not in his jurisdiction. A hitherto obscure official, the Official Solicitor, was enabled to intervene and the dockers were released. Strike followed strike. A miner on picket duty was accidentally killed. There was growing bitterness.

At the Treasury Mr Barber was tackling the problems of declining economic activity and growing unemployment with the now classical methods of Keynesian practice. He reduced taxation and increased domestic purchasing power. His policy was to spend Britain's way out of trouble and aim for a five per cent annual growth. On 23 June, the decision was made to float the pound, one of the most revolutionary acts of policy since the war. It eliminated devaluation as a solemn act, but left the pound vulnerable to the day-to-day decisions of the world currency markets.

During May the *Queen Elizabeth II*, a prestige transatlantic liner built to carry passengers who were now turning to air transport, received a threat in mid-Atlantic that a bomb would be exploded if a ransom of 350,000 dollars was not paid. At risk were the lives of 2,400 passengers and crew. The reaction in Britain was brilliant. A team of bomb-disposal experts were parachuted in the ocean near the ship, boarded her and after a search found nothing. Later in New York a man was given a long prison sentence for the pretence.

In May the Queen and Prince Philip played their part in 'the historic decision' to join Europe. They paid a state visit to France and were royally entertained by de Gaulle's successor, President Pompidou. The welcome seemed to mark a change from the hostility fostered with implacable hostility, disguised with the manners of a *grand seigneur*, of de Gaulle.

In Paris the Queen went to see her uncle, the Duke of Windsor, who was seventy-seven and failing in health. He died shortly after. His body was brought back and buried, after a service in St George's Chapel at Windsor, in the family mausoleum at Frogmore. The Duchess stayed at Buckingham Palace for the first time.

In the worst air crash in Britain 118 were killed when a BEA Trident crashed soon after take-off from London Airport.

The Olympic Games were held at Munich. The cost of the elaborate new buildings and stadia made it clear that only a handful of very rich nations would ever be able to be hosts to the Games. Palestinian Arab terrorists kidnapped Israeli athletes and eleven of them died when German police in a ham-handed operation tried to free them. In London an Israeli diplomat was killed by a letter bomb.

In July Mr Reginald Maudling, the Home Secretary and one of the most influential members of the Government, resigned to avoid any embarrassment to the police, for whom he was as minister responsible, in the investigation of former business associates who were involved in 'the Poulson affair'. Poulson was an energetic entrepreneur-architect who had built up a great business on bribery and corruption of civil servants, local government councillors and officials. The result was the trial and sentencing of a number of men prominent in public life. The circumstances warranted, in the opinion of the government, the setting up of a royal commission to examine all aspects of the behaviour of politicians and officials in the course of their duties.

The Queen's young cousin, Prince William of Gloucester, was killed in August when piloting a small private aircraft. His younger brother, Prince Richard, an architect, became Duke of Gloucester when his father died in 1974.

A 'cod war' broke out with Iceland this year. The dispute was over the rights of the British fishing fleet off the island. In this round of the conflict Iceland unilaterally declared a fifty-mile exclusive area off its shores. In law, it was in the wrong. But Britain's case was morally weakened by its assumption of rights to oil and gas far out into the North Sea.

At the Conservative conference Mr Heath, although he had won the election and relentlessly pushed through the official policy, still did not get the welcome accorded to Mr Enoch Powell. His brilliant oratory, directed this year at the Asians who were attempting on their British passports to enter Britain when General Amin evicted them from Uganda, and his call for a return to private enterprise, won him ecstatic applause.

In October the Queen went to Yugoslavia, the first Communist country she had visited. Marshal Tito and his people gave her a great welcome. She looked as if she was enjoying the magnificent scenery and the hospitality.

Mr Ian Smith arrested Mr Garfield Todd, a former Premier of Southern Rhodesia, and his daughter, Judith. They had been working for a compromise settlement. Compromise was not a permitted word in the language of Smith and his followers.

Nearly three hundred children had been born in Britain in the early sixties limbless or badly deformed as a result of their mothers taking the drug Thalidomide during their pregnancies. The company concerned, Distillers, offered compensation which was rejected as unsatisfactory. The *Sunday Times* played a notable part in finally securing adequate payments.

In November the Queen and Prince Philip celebrated their Silver Wedding anniversary. There was a school holiday, a drive through London, a service in Westminster Abbey where they had been married, and a great banquet given at Guildhall by the Lord Mayor.

The Conservative rank and file may have been spoiling for a show-down with the unions, but Mr Heath this year re-assessed his policy in the light of his experience in office and his responsibility as prime minister to the nation.

Mr Wilson had tried and failed to implement a voluntary wages and prices policy, although the unions would have been considered his normal allies. Now Mr Heath tried. He called a meeting of government, the unions and industry. This alone showed the extent of the change in his thinking.

He had been against government involvement in establishing rules. Now he asked, in his turn, for a voluntary system of wage and price control. The attempt failed.

In November Mr Heath resolutely froze all increases in pay, prices, rents and dividends for ninety days, with a possible sixty-day extension.

In the United States President Nixon had a spectacularly successful year. He visited Russia and China in an attempt to break out of the straitjacket of post-war American policies towards the Communist regimes. He toiled to bring an end to the Vietnam war. He was rewarded at the end of the year when he was re-elected to a second term with an overwhelming majority. He stood at the peak of power as a world statesman guiding the course of future history.

Apollo 16 and *17* – the last in the series of American space exploration – travelled to and from the moon.

On 1 January 1973 Britain formally joined the Common Market. There was some celebration and a number of events and exhibitions entitled, 'Fanfare for Europe'.

It was a great day for Mr Heath, but it would be wrong to say there was any great enthusiasm. It was a worrying time. The mood of organized labour was bitter. Industry felt a sense of injustice as prices were held down while costs rose.

In the shops prices were rising, in spite of government measures. Food was particularly affected and the Common Market came in for a lot of the blame.

In Brussels, the Common Market headquarters, disagreements soon broke out between Britain and the old members of the Community.

Anthony Barber produced a neutral budget, with some anti-inflationary measures. But the policy of Mr Heath was still for growth. A series of phased wage increases was authorized to compensate for the rising inflation.

In May there was a call-girl scandal which led to the resignation of two ministers. Anthony Lambton, who had given up the title of Earl of Durham to continue a career in the House of Commons, admitted frequenting call-girls. Earl Jellicoe, Lord Privy Seal and Leader of the House of Lords, had also used girls from escort agencies.

What would have been considered peccadilloes elsewhere were punished harshly. It meant the end of two notable careers in public life.

Princess Anne became engaged at the end of May to Captain Mark Phillips of the Queen's Dragoon Guards. He was a horseman of Olympic Games standards. Their mutual interest in horses had brought them together. Anne had shown herself by now a young woman of decided views and a certain impatience. She had twice been stopped for driving at over seventy mph on motorways. She likes fox-hunting and says so. She has her troubles with the press. Like her father in his younger days she sometimes does not understand that photographers and reporters are, like her, doing a job, and that the royal family, monarchy itself, is dependent on coverage by the media.

In September Prince Philip went with his daughter to Soviet Russia, where she was taking part in the international riding championships. The visit had its significance. It was the first time the British royal family had set foot in the country since the 1917 Revolution – fifty-six years before.

As Queen of Australia, a new title omitting any reference to Britain, the Queen went to Sydney to open the great Opera House which had been so many years building. It can rank as one of the wonders of the world. The Queen had a great welcome although the prime minister, Mr Gough Whitlam, leading a moderately left-wing government, was stressing independence rather stridently.

In the Middle East the economies of not only Britain, but of all the industrialized countries were threatened by rises in the price of oil which by the end of the year would reach four hundred per cent. The oil-producing countries, linked in OPEC, had ended the epoch of cheap oil and helped to plunge the world into the worst recession since the thirties. The new huge oil revenues would change the economic and, consequently, the political balance of the world.

The Anglo–American oil companies, 'the Seven Sisters', which had for so long controlled the world market, were virtually powerless and awaiting nationalization of their production. Their governments could not defend them by force without risking world war.

The Common Market was perturbed by a decision made at the Labour party conference that if it came to power it would first renegotiate better terms and then give the British a final say in an election or a referendum.

On 6 October Egyptian and Syrian forces launched a surprise attack against Israel on *Yom Kippur*, the Day of the Atonement, one of the most sacred days in the Jewish calendar.

Israel was nearly overwhelmed by forces equipped with sophisticated Russian weapons. The United States rushed in supplies to help its ally. The crisis was overcome and by the time of an imposed cease-fire the Israelis were fighting back with increasing success.

The Middle East oil countries, as a consequence, imposed another oil embargo . . . this time directed particularly against the United States and Holland, as friends of Israel.

By November a shortage of both coal and oil was developing in Britain. On the thirteenth a state of emergency was declared. The trade figures were alarming. Bank rate was put up to an unprecedented thirteen per cent. There was panic selling on the Stock Exchange. Industrial strife was continuing and the Industrial Relations Court, which had now sequestrated some union assets as a punishment, was accused of being a political court.

It was in this atmosphere that Princess Anne was married to Mark Phillips in Westminster Abbey. However, it was a touch of colourful glamour which for a few hours relieved the TV screens of its tales of woe.

The crisis deepened. There were disputes with the railway workers and, more ominously, the miners were taking up position with a ban on overtime.

By December Sir Michael Clapham, president of the CBI, was telling Mr Heath to prepare for the worst, abandon his growth policy and concentrate on national survival. Even Conservative opinion was pressing for harsh economic measures, including a rise in income tax.

On 13 December Mr Heath renewed the state of emergency and announced that as from 31 December there would be a three-day week to save fuel. Mr Barber a few days later produced a mini-budget which cut government expenditure. But such was the feeling in the City and industry that the measures were criticized for not being tough enough. The cry was for the government to govern, whatever the consequences.

Ulster still contributed its daily tale of murder and arson. Arab guns were being used in London in attempted assassinations of prominent Jews.

The year was moving to a bad end, with prospects of worse to come.

There were many by this time who wondered if the institutions of the country would be strong enough to take the strain. There were some, on both the extreme right and extreme left, who were hoping they would not.

It was not an easy year for the Queen as she watched and listened. There is a very special danger for the British crown when a bitter economic-political struggle comes to a head. For the right tends to identify the monarchy with its sectional interests at such a time.

That way lies disaster.

TEN

Politics, finances and celebrations

The year 1974 started in an atmosphere of crisis and conditions became worse as the effects of the three-day week bit into the life of the nation. The immediate problem for Mr Heath was to solve the miners' wages dispute. A meeting on 14 January at 10, Downing Street broke down. On 4 February a last attempt was made and failed.

Mr Heath called a general election. Considering the extraordinary circumstances it was conducted in a calm manner. Mr Heath's message was: 'It is time for you to say to the extremists, the militants and plain and simple misguided, we've had enough.' Labour said, 'Get Britain Back To Work.'

Mr Enoch Powell said he was going to vote Labour because it had promised to take a second look at the Common Market. Sir Campbell Adamson, director-general of the CBI said the Industrial Relations Act – the corner-stone of Mr Heath's industrial policy – should be repealed. Many Conservatives felt that with friends like that it was better to deal with the enemy.

Labour just won. But Mr Heath, tenacious of power, stayed at No. 10 while he tried to get Mr Jeremy Thorpe and his handful of Liberals to join a coalition. But the Liberals declined to keep the Conservatives in power. That decision explains much of their future attitude to Thorpe and his colleagues.

In the new atmosphere of a Labour government wage demands were settled. By 8 March the nation was back on a five-day week. There were

At Aberfan, South Wales in October 1966. A slag-heap fell on the mining village engulfing a school and killing 144, mainly children. The Queen said to the parents on her visit, 'All I can give is my comfort and sympathy.' But she, followed by the nation and friends abroad, gave generously to the disaster fund.

OPPOSITE ABOVE Concorde was taking shape at Filton when the Queen paid a visit in 1966. A technological triumph, it was nevertheless to be ten years and hundreds of millions of pounds later before the supersonic passenger planes of the Anglo-French project went into scheduled service.

OPPOSITE BELOW The Post Office Tower in London, 1966. Behind the Queen is Anthony Wedgwood Benn, then Postmaster General.

ABOVE An expert eye. The Crown Jewels had been given a better display in the Tower of London.

LEFT Improved communications centre at New Scotland Yard which she toured.

BELOW A jolly tea party at Pooles Park Primary School, North London.
RIGHT Making faces.
BOTTOM At Expo '67 in Canada with Mr Lester Pearson, the Prime Minister. The royal family came over later in force.

A night at the Opera House. Princess Margaret and Lord Snowdon make up the family party.

The Queen addresses her learned Judges, led by the Lord Chancellor, Lord Gardiner. She was opening a large extension to the Law Courts in London, 1968, made necessary largely by the increase in divorces.

ABOVE The RAF's Golden Jubilee display in 1968 at Abingdon, Berkshire. This is the Vickers Gunbus, the earliest armed aircraft to fly with the then Royal Flying Corps in the 1914–18 war. 'Only the planes have changed,' said Tom Aldous, a veteran of those days, 'the spirit is the same.'

LEFT A morning ride with Princess Margaret and the Duke of Kent at Ascot before the professionals start racing in the afternoon.

OPPOSITE ABOVE 21 April 1968. The Queen's birthday. She was 42. The picture was taken in the grounds of Windsor Castle.

OPPOSITE BELOW Trooping the Colour, 1971.

The Opening of Parliament, October 1969. With the Queen is Prince Charles, whom she had earlier in the year invested as Prince of Wales at Caernarvon Castle.

The Commonwealth Prime Ministers' Conference of 1969. The Queen is Head of a Commonwealth that has largely come into being during her reign.

increased taxes in the budget and £500m more for food subsidies. A total freeze on all house and flat rents destroyed at a stroke a vast speculative situation which had been built up in the property market.

Vast profits had been made. Now vast losses were incurred. The City was near to collapse. This was the 'secondary bank' crisis which was only solved by the patient rescue work of the Bank of England, which was to last years.

Many of the 'whiz-kids', who had been multi-millionaires with an apparently infallible Midas touch, were destroyed. The old City establishment shed few tears over them for in their arrogant days they had made enemies.

The Labour government gave priority to dismantling the Industrial Relations Act. Its court came to an end after a final flurry of judgments against unions. Mr Wilson buried 'the putrefying corpse of Tory legislation'.

But it was difficult to remain confident about the situation. The world recession was striking at international trade. Exporting was becoming more difficult. There was heavy unemployment in the two industrial leaders, the United States and Germany. It was a time for retrenchment. But for the new British government this was politically impossible.

In March a daring attempt was made to kidnap Princess Anne as she was returning to the Palace with her husband after an evening function. Although planned and executed by only one man – who was afterwards found insane – it might well have succeeded. The motive was money – a ransom of £3m to be paid in used five pound notes. The man halted the royal car in the Mall. He was armed and in a struggle shot the Princess's police guard three times. Finally he was pinned down. Inspector James Beaton survived his wounds and was awarded the George Cross, a very high award indeed. It was not only an honour to him, but to the entire police force which was at this time enduring considerable danger from armed gangs of one sort or another.

Marcia Williams, an able and not unattractive woman, who had for some years occupied an influential position in British politics as Mr Wilson's political secretary, was in the news in 1974. She was a divorced woman who later had two children by a Fleet Street political journalist.

During 1974 the press discovered that Marcia Williams's brother, Mr Anthony Field, who at one time had been in charge of Mr Wilson's personal staff, had made substantial profits from land transactions – the area which the Labour government had vehemently criticized and attacked. Some of the profits had been for his sister's benefit.

The prime minister defended Marcia, her brother and the transactions. He said there was a great difference between land speculation and land reclamation – the deals had concerned the rehabilitation of old slag-heaps. The Conservatives made the most they could of the situation and even among Mr Wilson's supporters there was a sense of distaste.

But Mr Wilson went further. On 24 May he made Marcia a life-peer. She took her seat in the House of Lords as Lady Falkender.

In June the Prince of Wales made his maiden speech in the House of Lords. It was a long time since a royal Duke had spoken there. He chose a politically neutral subject – the need for better co-ordination of leisure facilities. He spoke well and the Lords applauded the heir to the throne with more than politeness.

Since then the Prince has made television appearances on a variety of subjects – his ancestor, King George III, and Canterbury Cathedral – and a wider public has appreciated his talents.

He is acquiring his own style. The slightly amused diffidence of his early years is giving way to an assured ease. He makes sure he knows what he is talking about.

Cyprus was invaded by the Turkish army in July. The action had long been threatened to defend the flouted rights of the Turkish minority. The action ended with the virtual partition of the island. It also led to the end of the military junta in Greece after seven years of brutal dictatorship.

On 8 August President Nixon resigned and Gerald Ford, the vice-president took over. The world had watched on its television screens the relentless investigation of the Watergate affair which destroyed Nixon.

The American presidency had been growing in power steadily since Roosevelt assumed almost dictatorial powers in the thirties to combat the Great Depression. The Watergate affair gave Congress its opportunity to restore the balance.

The moral and physical decay of the man who had but a short time before stood on a pinnacle of world power was a tragedy of Sophoclean proportions.

In August the giant holiday firm Court Line collapsed and brought difficulties to over 150,000 people who were on holiday or had paid deposits. Other firms in the industry were also in trouble.

It was a setback to a remarkable industry which has enabled millions of ordinary British men and women to enjoy a holiday in the sun and in exotic surroundings that would have been an impossible dream a generation before.

The troubles of the industry have been overcome and the package holiday is now available with greater safeguards – but the recession has reduced the traffic for the time being.

Another dictatorship fell in August. The Portuguese 'Revolution of the Flowers' was led by officers of the armies which had had the unenviable and finally impossible task of holding down liberation movements in the African colonies of Mozambique and Angola. It was enlivening, to say the least, to see a revolution led by an officer corps which was imbued with Marxism.

The new government promised independence to Mozambique and Angola. This was to lead to basic changes in the power structure of Central and Southern Africa which was to have its effect on Rhodesia and South Africa.

It happened at a time when, in fact, South Africa was pursuing vigorously a policy of improving relations with the new states of Africa – with some success. It was also tending to keep Rhodesia more at arm's length.

The Queen and her advisers had much to consider in the government's September White Paper on the devolution of powers in Scotland and Wales. It followed a royal commission on the subject which advocated great changes.

With promise of oil off Scottish coasts turning into reality, the Scottish Nationalist Party, for long dismissed as romantic and slightly loony, had become a power. In the February election it did very well indeed, mainly at the expense of the Conservatives. Hard-headed Scots jumped on a band-waggon that promised wealth as well as increased political power. Talk of independence from England, once a monopoly of poets' pubs, was heard in the drawing-rooms of shrewd Edinburgh lawyers.

The Scottish Stuarts, by succeeding to the Tudors in England had united the two thrones. A Scotland considering independence could threaten this united monarchy.

The Queen holds a short court each year at Holyroodhouse in the late summer. The royal family spends a long autumn holiday most years at Balmoral. But the once fervid enthusiasm of the Scots for the monarchy, largely engendered by Victoria and Albert, has declined this century with the passing of the semi-feudal power structure of aristocrats and retainers. That the Queen has the bagpipes played under her window when she breakfasts find no appreciative echo with the new-style nationalists.

They see the chance of sweeping the board in a general election and holding either Conservatives or Labour to ransom at Westminster.

The Welsh have, as yet, no oil off their coasts to back their desire for greater independence. But a fierce love of their country, their language and their culture is to be reckoned with. For the monarchy, it is now more than ever significant that a male heir to the throne is traditionally the Prince of Wales.

At the beginning of October there was another general election, but if Mr Wilson had hoped for a secure mandate, he was disappointed. Labour came back with a precarious majority and dependent on the support of minority groups. The only memorable statement was by Mr Denis Healey, the Chancellor of the Exchequer, who said that inflation was running at the rate of 8·4 per cent. Robert Carr said the figure was around 22 per cent. At the end of the year it was officially estimated at 18·3 per cent. It has been difficult since then to give much credence to Mr Healey.

In an emergency November budget Mr Healey reflated the economy with £1,500 million for industry. An extra £600 million spending power was created. The weekly wage rate had gone up by 20·8 per cent in a year. But living standards had now been falling for several years. Business reported a growing lack of confidence. It was an ominous time.

At the end of November Mr John Stonehouse, a Labour MP, who had proved himself an able minister before going into business, disappeared off a Miami beach, apparently drowned. It was the beginning of a story alleging fraud, theft and forgery on a considerable and ingenious scale. It also had a sex interest as Mr Stonehouse's attractive secretary and mistress was involved.

Just before Christmas he was picked up by the Melbourne police. He was brought back to Britain to face charges.

On 28 December the Queen and Prince Philip moved into Wood Farm, a six-bedroom farmhouse on the royal estate at Sandringham for four weeks. The big house itself was being reconstructed at a cost of £200,000.

In 1975 Britain came so close to disaster that the world held its breath. In June inflation was running at the rate of 36·4 per cent, making a nonsense of the economy and generating so grave a situation that calls for a government of national survival with wide powers found a considerable response.

It was no use this time blaming the City or the trade unions or the gnomes of Zurich; successive governments had failed to tell the people the truth about the British economy and take the necessary measures. It was the politicians who were to blame – going back a long time.

The hero of the hour was Mr Jack Jones of the Transport and General Workers' Union. A small, quietly-spoken, austere man of convinced socialist views he led a campaign to get the trade unions to accept a £6 a week flat rate maximum increase. He succeeded.

Without that measure Britain's foreign creditors, friends and allies, could well have abandoned the country to its fate.

By November inflation was down to 14·9 per cent. A measure of confidence was cautiously expressed abroad.

This was the story of 1975 and the Queen was in a position to observe it with all the detailed information available to her.

In January the Duke of Norfolk, a close friend of the royal family, died surrounded with an affectionate respect which was a remarkable achievement for an aristocrat who never departed by an iota from his devotion to tradition.

Hereditary Earl Marshal, a grandee in Sussex where Arundel Castle seemed the centre of a ducal fief, an authority in the Jockey Club and the MCC, he could have been a subject of caricature with his pompous looks and voice. But he was a shrewd man, learned how to deal with the media, and did his best, according to his opportunities, which were considerable, to preserve what he thought was the worthwhile heritage of the past.

His ancestors had been warriors and schemers, with kingdoms and their heads at stake. His role had been ceremonial and advisory. The fighting and the scheming was now in other hands . . . among them those of Jack Jones, who despises royal Ascot where the Duke had been master.

In February the Queen asked Parliament for another increase. The Civil List was raised by £420,000 to £1,400,000. In view of the economic situation the Queen offered to meet £150,000 of the extra costs for one year. She also suspended the modernizing of Sandringham.

The same month she went round several centres in London to meet the men and women who were responsible for dealing with bomb outrages and their casualties. She visited Scotland Yard, the London Fire Brigade Headquarters, the London Ambulance Headquarters and the South-West District Post Office at Victoria. The next month she paid similar visits in Birmingham which had also suffered from bombings.

If she gets bored at times dubbing as knights worthy, but not remarkable men, she had an opportunity at this time to honour an authentic genius, Charlie Chaplin.

Mrs Margaret Thatcher was elected leader of the Conservative Party, defeating Mr Heath in a first ballot with surprising ease. Conservative MP's had for some time been expressing their dissatisfaction with Edward Heath, who had lost three out of the four elections held while he was leader. But the result was a humiliation from which he has found difficulty in recovering.

The renegotiation of the terms on which Britain had entered the Common Market proceeded with vigour. On 11 March 1975 agreement on new terms was reached at a summit meeting in Dublin. Arrangements were set in motion for a referendum and in the following months a great public debate was held, exhaustive and exhausting. The result of the referendum on 5 June was a decisive two-to-one vote in favour of joining. The long, long debate was over.

The Vietnam war was ending. The Americans had withdrawn, leaving vast material. The corrupt puppet government was finding its armies would no longer fight. Saigon fell to the Communists and the Americans did more than their best to evacuate some of those whose lives would be forfeit. One could only wish the Vietnamese well, whatever their government, after an ordeal which had started when as a French colony they were occupied by the Japanese, then involved in a successful fight against the French when they came back and finally devastated by the Americans who came to pre-serve democracy.

In April the Queen went to Jamaica for a four-day visit which coincided with a Commonwealth conference there. She gave a dinner to thirty-three Commonwealth leaders on *Britannia*, which lay at anchor in Kingston Harbour. It was an imaginative use of the royal yacht, for the occasion on board symbolized the world-wide associations of the Commonwealth at a time when Britain was creating other links in the Common Market.

The British motor-car industry, as represented by British Leyland, had for some time been sinking into decay, plagued by industrial disputes and a management that did not manage. Sir Don (later Lord) Ryder had been asked to see what could be done. His report said that £1,500m of public funds would have to be invested over seven years. The report had to be accepted. Too many jobs and the future of the industry were at stake. It was another dismal chapter in the story of British industry. Earlier Ferranti's, the electronics firm, and Burmah Oil, had joined the queue for public money to bail them out.

Early in May the Queen and Prince Philip returned the state visit of the Emperor of Japan. The trip gave them an opportunity of going to Hong Kong, a flourishing crown colony, known mainly as a centre of the drug trade and an exporter of cheap goods produced by sweated labour.

Back in London the Queen installed the Prince of Wales as Great Master of the Order of the Bath in the King Henry VII Chapel of Westminster Abbey. In June she was, as usual, at the Derby and Ascot. She opened a fine new extension of the National Gallery, the New Covent Garden market across the river and went to Stratford-upon-Avon to see a gala performance of Shakespeare.

The royal visits to Scotland were this year noticeably more significant, showing an appreciation of the new situation there. Installed in Holyroodhouse, the Queen gave lunch to the Knights of the Thistle, the Scottish equivalent of the Garter. The Queen Mother was there and followed by the Prince of Wales and Princess Margaret. A series of visits was made in the royal train. Then the King of Sweden arrived in Scotland to begin his state visit to Britain. There was some pomp and ceremony and a reunion of the Scottish regiments in Holyrood Park.

Early in November the Queen was back in Scotland to perform one of the most important functions of her reign. At Aberdeen she symbolically turned on the first major flow of oil from the North Sea. It was from British Petroleum's Forties Field.

It was a triumph for American and British technology. The huge amounts of money needed to exploit the fields had also come from many sources. But the benefits to Britain would be great. By 1980 enough oil would be flowing for self-sufficiency and even some for export. There would be great savings of foreign currency. The irony of the situation was that if the Arabs had not pushed up the price of oil so high, the costs of North Sea oil would have been wildly uneconomic.

With ample gas already flowing from the North Sea farther south, with great indigenous coal reserves, Britain could look to a future energy independence that was the envy of many industrial countries. The question was – did the country possess politicians of the calibre to make good use of the advantages provided by technology?

In Spain General Franco, the Fascist leader of his country for nearly forty years, died and was succeeded, as he had arranged, by Prince Juan Carlos of the Spanish royal family. The new King and his Queen, Sophia, a Greek princess, are related to the Queen and Prince Philip. His task of restoring a democracy is difficult, but he has powerful friends, including the Americans.

The Queen found herself involved in a constitutional crisis in Australia. Her representative, the Governor-General, Sir John Kerr, dismissed the prime minister, Mr Gough Whitlam, and called a general election which resulted in a victory for Mr Malcolm Fraser, leading a Liberal party that would be considered Conservative in Britain. Sir John's action is still hotly debated. Did he involve the crown in politics?

President Nyerere of Tanzania came for a state visit in November. It was a good sign for the Commonwealth because Tanzania, since its independence, had pursued under Nyerere a policy that had tended to link it with Communist countries, especially China.

Portugal withdrew from its African colonies. The hand-over went smoothly in Mozambique, but in Angola rival parties were in conflict and the victory of the MPLA was effected with the aid of Cuban troops.

Lord Ryder became the head of the National Enterprise Board, set up by the government to increase enterprise in industry. Chrysler's, the American car makers who were in world-wide difficulties, managed to secure £162·5m aid from the British government to save its local subsidiary. The action was taken reluctantly to save jobs when unemployment was rising. The Sex Discrimination and Equal Pay Acts came into force at the end of the year.

But just before Christmas Mr Wilson saw through Parliament the Civil List Act which arranged for the Queen's requests for money to be put before the House annually in the same way as any other public expenditure.

The purpose was to keep up with inflation.

In return the Queen took over the allowances paid to the Duke of Kent, Princess Alexandra, the Duke of Gloucester and Princess Alice, Countess of Athlone. These would amount to £120,000 in 1976.

In future the Civil List will provide only for the sovereign, the consort of the sovereign and for the children of a sovereign and their widows.

The measure went through the House of Commons smoothly enough. Apart from loyalty and affection, it was recognized that the standards of the Queen and those of her family who help her in the royal duties, must be maintained. But the British could be forgiven a sigh of envy as they cut back their standard of living.

On 21 January 1976 the British and French Concordes started regular scheduled passenger flights. The British went to Bahrein; the French to South America. After so many years, so much treasure, so many misgivings, it was good to see them in service. Their future may be in doubt, their noise unacceptable, but there was a certain pride in Britain – and probably more in France. It was an achievement to be proud of.

Peter Hain was in the news again when he was arrested on a charge of seizing a bundle of notes from a bank near his home in Putney. The evidence of identification was discredited and he was acquitted. It led to widespread doubt on identification evidence and some men serving sentences were released on the authority of Mr Jenkins, the Home Secretary. Police rules were examined critically.

But the Hain case had other repercussions. Allegations were made that the South African security agency, Boss, had framed him as a reprisal for his anti-apartheid activities.

Prince Bernhard of the Netherlands was mentioned as a recipient of bribes from Lockheed, the American aircraft manufacturers, whose business methods were being investigated in the United States. The company's activities involved many highly-placed men, including a former Japanese prime minister, Mr Tanaka, who was later arrested. In Holland a commission was set up to enquire into the allegations against Prince Bernhard. The affair has grieved the Dutch for the royal House of Orange enjoys a very deep loyalty, based on the fact that its independence was won by its Princes.

In Britain unemployment was rising to well over a million. The £6 pay limit was holding. Inflation was coming down – but not quickly enough.

The Queen was given another increase – £500,000. It went through under the new arrangements with scarcely a word. The Queen's civil list now stood at £1,900,000 p.a.

On 16 March Mr Wilson, a few days after his sixtieth birthday, went to the Palace and told the Queen that he was resigning as soon as the Parliamentary Labour Party had elected a new leader. She was not surprised. He had told her the previous December that he would be giving up shortly. The Cabinet and the country, however, were taken aback. There were so many critical decisions to be taken.

The favourite candidate, Mr James Callaghan, sixty-four, who had filled most of the great offices of state, was elected leader and the Queen asked him to form a government.

On 19 March Buckingham Palace announced that Princess Margaret, 45, and Lord Snowdon, 46, were separating. 'The Queen,' it said, 'is naturally very sad at what has happened. There has been no pressure from the Queen on either Princess Margaret or Lord Snowdon to take any particular course.'

Lord Snowdon, who behaved with great dignity, said he was 'desperately sad' and appealed for understanding for the two children.

That the marriage had been breaking down was common knowledge. So, thanks to a less inhibited press, was her friendship with Roderick Llewellyn, an attractive young man of twenty-eight.

The Queen was fifty on 21 April. She gave a dinner party, mainly for family, at Windsor the evening before, followed by a ball for five hundred. The next day she gave a reception for the 180 heroic members of the Victoria Cross and George Cross Association.

Princess Anne had a bad fall at a Horse Trials meeting and suffered concussion. She was training hard to get a place in the British equestrian team for the Montreal Olympic Games in July.

The Queen created Harold Wilson and the Duke of Grafton, a great land-owner in East Anglia, Knights of the Garter. They were duly installed at Windsor in St George's Chapel in June.

On 6 May the government and the TUC agreed in principle on another year of wage restraint to follow the £6 limit. This time it was 4½ per cent – a minimum of £2·50 and a maximum of £4 a week with small, but welcome tax reliefs in the budget. It was an astonishing achievement and once again Mr Jack Jones was in the van for acceptance. There was a political price to pay, however, in this close alliance between the government and the TUC. At its special conference held later to confirm the agreement, Mr Sidney Weighell, the railwaymen's leader, spelled it out: 'We are in a powerful position. Nobody can govern in Britain without our acquiescence.'

Mr Jeremy Thorpe resigned on 10 May the leadership of the Liberal Party he had held with great success since 1967. For months he had faced accusations that he had had a homosexual relationship with Mr Norman Scott, a former male model, whom he had befriended. Once again, there were allegations that the South African security agency had been at work and had been involved in prosecuting the campaign against Mr Thorpe.

Sir Harold Wilson's resignation honours list, which had been for some weeks accurately leaked in the press, was finally published. It was bitterly attacked by Mr George Hutchinson, a political commentator of *The Times*, who accused Lady Falkender of having influenced the list. She replied at length saying she had had nothing to do with it.

Princess Anne bemoaned her fate in an article published in the British Airways publication, *High Life*. 'We've never had a holiday,' she was quoted as saying, 'A week at Balmoral or ten days at Sandringham is the nearest we get.' She went on to say that she found sight-seeing 'purgatory'. 'You seldom see anything; either too many people or too many press.'

Her remarks were no help to her mother. They were no help to the politicians of both major parties who have in recent years stressed that the allowances paid to the royal family (Princess Anne after her marriage receives £35,000 p.a.) are no more than an expense account to defray the costs incurred in carrying out duties.

However, a few weeks later the Princess should have been consoled. The Queen bought her a Cotswold estate for £700,000. It covers 730 acres, has a charming eighteenth-century mansion and ample stables in need of repair.

Just before Mr Vorster, the South African prime minister, was due to fly to Germany for talks with Dr Kissinger, the American Secretary of State, serious riots broke out in Soweto, a black African township of around a million inhabitants outside Johannesburg. Around two hundred were killed by the white security forces and over a thousand wounded. The rioting spread to other townships, but was speedily dealt with. The ostensible cause of the outbreak was the compulsory teaching of Afrikaans. The real cause was the anger of the black population, simmering under apartheid.

The talks with Dr Kissinger brought little comfort to Mr Vorster. The Secretary of State had recently visited Africa and proclaimed in firm terms that the United States was on the side of black Africa.

In Rhodesia the situation was steadily worsening. Mr Smith had talks with African nationalist leaders, but nothing of value came of them. A few ineffective reforms were made internally. Mr Garfield Todd was released from house arrest.

But an armed campaign against Rhodesia was spreading from the long border with Mozambique. From scarce foreign currency Rhodesia was buying arms and recruiting mercenaries. Meanwhile, some young Rhodesians were leaving to find a more secure future elsewhere.

In spite of the new pay deal the pound began to slide. This helped the exports and tourist trade, but made imports more expensive and reduced the chances of reaching the target of single-figure inflation by the end of the year (the rate was 13·8 per cent in July). Pressure was built up outside, especially by America, for cuts in government expenditure, although it was not high in relation to output with other Western European countries.

The pressure from outside reinforced Conservative demands. Mrs Thatcher's front bench may have been 'composed of nobodies who stand for nothing and impress no one', but circumstances were in their favour by the summer.

Unemployment was over one and a half million and included many school-leavers. Prices were still going up in the shops. Mr Michael Foot as Labour's Leader of the House seemed to many to be riding roughshod over Parliament to push through the nationalization of shipbuilding and the aircraft industry. The government was felt to be soft in controlling illegal immigration and there were outbreaks of racism. In the few by-elections held the Labour vote was low and the Conservative high. In the House of Commons the government's majority was daily more precarious.

To bolster sterling a stand-by credit of $5,000m was arranged, mainly by America and Germany. But the price was cuts. Mr Healey told Labour that if they were not made, the government would fall and the Conservatives would inherit the North Sea oil revenues and the benefits of an improving world trade situation.

The cuts were made. They totalled nearly £2,000m for 1977–8. £1,012m from government departments; £910m from a two per cent increase in employers' national insurance contributions. This last measure infuriated the CBI. Its leader, Lord Watkinson, a man of imposing statesmanship, felt Mr Callaghan had broken faith with previous assurances to industry and said so.

The Queen received the French president, M. Giscard d'Estaing, who during his state visit gave the British an opportunity of admiring his handsome looks and brilliant intellect. He spent a day in Scotland, no doubt recalling 'The Auld Alliance' that had linked the two countries in the past.

The Communists had a great meeting in Berlin and Mr Brezhnev the Soviet leader, had to listen to many national parties expressing their determination to go it alone – a development which must have pleased the aged Marshal Tito who attended. One of the most outspoken was Signor Berlinguer, leader of the Italian Communist Party. However, it did not emerge in the Italian general election as the ruling party. But it did consolidate its position as the second force in the land. The German Chancellor later admitted that if the Communists had won there would have been no financial help for ailing Italy.

The Israelis, in a brilliantly conceived and executed commando raid, freed over a hundred of its citizens held hostage by Palestinian Arabs at Entebbe airport in Uganda, with the apparent support of its President Amin.

Princess Alexandra's husband, Angus Ogilvy, was criticized in a Department of Trade report on the affairs of Lonhro, the international trading company, of which he had long been a director. Mr Ogilvy announced that he would be resigning all his directorships, but strongly rebutted the report.

Britain enjoyed – or suffered – a prolonged heat-wave and experienced a severe drought in many areas. The Arabs were continuing to buy property in London on a large scale; one of their acquisitions was the Dorchester Hotel. Rabies became an increasing threat from Europe. Many Britons sighed at their finances and abandoned all hope of the accustomed holiday.

The Queen and Prince Philip went to the USA for the two hundredth celebrations of its independence and then on to Montreal to open the Olympic Games. She looked splendid. The years have, as happens with other lucky women, given her a beauty not there before. She walks well. Her clothes are just right. Her speeches, which are now on important occasions very much her own, said something worthwhile.

In Independence Hall at Philadelphia, the seat of the revolution, she said: 'We lost the American colonies because we lacked that statesmanship "to know the right time and the manner of yielding what is impossible to keep."'

Bob Hope, at the presidential banquet in the White House, consoled her and all the British when he said, referring to the American acquisition of many British possessions, including the old liner Queen Mary and London Bridge, 'You have not so much lost a colony as found an annexe.'

In Montreal she had with her not only her husband, but her three sons, the Prince of Wales, Prince Andrew and Prince Edward, all there to see Princess Anne, who had won her place in the British equestrian team.

Talking to the Canadian people, conscious of the difficulties between the English- and French-speaking communities, she said, 'It is not an easy thing for peoples of different cultural traditions and speaking two different languages to live together and share the same political traditions.'

She said of the Canadian confederation: 'To preserve it will demand vision, courage and generosity – all too rare in the present world.'

The words were to Canada. But the message was to the whole Commonwealth of which she is head.

ELEVEN

How has it been?

A Silver Jubilee is a good time to take stock. Twenty-five years is a considerable part of anyone's life; it is even an appreciable period in the life of a nation.

The Queen is fifty and her reign covers the last twenty-five years of the post-war era. The 1939–45 war was part of her life. Her husband served in the war. So did most of the men around her, officials, friends and, latterly, politicians.

Although she was only nineteen when the war ended, the climacteric for her and the men and women of her generation was the war. Although a fresh start had to be made – it could only be described as 'post-war'.

It was a time of hope for all, but especially for the young, full of energy and a desire for change. Elizabeth spoke in her twenty-first birthday broadcast of a Commonwealth – 'more free, more prosperous, more happy and a more powerful influence for good in the world than it has been in the greatest days of our forefathers'.

How has it been?

For Britain and the Commonwealth there has been no major war. The nuclear holocaust, more than once threatening, did not occur. Neither Britain nor the Commonwealth had a say in that. It was the decision of the United States and Soviet Russia.

Until 1972, Elizabeth's reign was marked by a continuing and unprecedented prosperity for the majority of the British people that was after a time taken so much for granted, that its diminution has spread disproportionate dismay and discontent.

The Welfare State, the Consumer Society, the Permissive Society, were labels given to mark stages in a more secure, more free life, enjoyed by a healthier, better educated, better fed and better housed people. The churches may have been emptying, but the spirit abroad expressed more of the Christian ethic than when they were full.

These achievements happened in years of government by both Conservative and Labour parties.

But the world recession, the quadrupling of oil prices, inflation, business less profitable, unemployment rising has changed the picture. The old bitterness of a class-ridden society has emerged from the past as workers and employers try to pass the loss of living standards on to each other.

It is a time when the weak and unorganized go to the wall. But, fortunately, the welfare state has so far survived the attacks of those who would use the crisis as an excuse for destroying the measure of social justice created by men and women of goodwill of the main political parties.

The recent years have shown how persistent the forces of reaction are. The price of liberty, as Wendell Phillips remarked to the Massachusetts Anti-Slavery Society over a century ago, is eternal vigilance. The words can never be quoted enough.

A large measure of the progress was achieved by the handmaiden of mankind, technology. It would be stupid not to praise her successes, even if they have made her at times more mistress than maid. The politicians should be grateful, for the progress could be attributed to them, even though they have often more hindered than helped.

The British of all classes are a conservative people. But, in the Queen's reign, she has been able to observe the slow crumbling of the dominant position of the upper-middle class. The change is reflected in the manner of dress, of accent, of behaviour. It is reflected in the theatre, the dance and the popular press.

The culture is changing. The creative men and women, the architects, artists, writers and poets, who will give the flavour of the period to posterity, have reflected the atmosphere of transition. They are the primitives of what may, with luck, be a flowering renaissance.

In Britain the contribution of the coloured immigrants may well enrich this civilization with new aspects of truth and beauty.

All this the Queen can see as she observes the people over which she reigns.

It is said, rightly, that we are now one of the poorer nations of Western Europe. This, with better leadership, may well change. But it is worth recalling that when Britain was very rich and powerful, according to statistics, the lot of the majority was one of ignorance, insecurity, poor physique and narrow horizons.

Yet, withal these changes, empowered by technology, have been made peacefully. The people has given small majorities to both Conservative and

Labour governments. The nation, all classes, has made favourites on TV of such nostalgic series as *The Forsyte Saga*, *Dad's Army*, *Edward VII* and *Upstairs, Downstairs*.

The Queen has asked six men to form a government – Churchill was already prime minister when she came to the throne. The others have been – Eden, Macmillan, Douglas-Home, Wilson, Heath and Callaghan.

Macmillan and Wilson were very good by any standards. Conscious of tradition, they guided change. But they were not great leaders. Aneurin Bevan, Hugh Gaitskell, Iain Macleod, who all died too young, had given promise of greatness. If Macmillan had not been so determined to deprive R. A. Butler of the Premiership for reasons still obscure, it might have been different. Rab (now Lord) Butler had quietly created during the war as a member of the coalition the blueprint of the Welfare State that Attlee built. Under the manner of a cardinal-statesman of the renaissance, he was capable of vision as Adenauer and de Gaulle were. But the Queen's choice of prime minister, except in a very grave emergency, is limited by the parties' machinery, which tends to produce men who will be safe.

In the world outside Britain, the Queen has had more influence in shaping events than at home. For she has travelled as the representative not only of Britain as a nation but of the British idea. Her travels have been one of her great contributions, not only as Queen, but because as a person she has qualities that are admired – courtesy, charm and, increasingly, a quiet humour.

The great challenge in her reign has been the transformation of the British Empire into the Commonwealth. Not the British Commonwealth, but the Commonwealth. In this she has played an invaluable part.

It is something of a miracle that it exists. So many said it would break up. So many influences were brought to bear to make it break up. '*E pur si muove!*' It is exciting to look down the list, covering the world, of thirty-five independent, free states, members of the Commonwealth and acknowledging Elizabeth as Queen or Head.

An association of men and women of many colours, races, languages, religions, cultures, able to meet, talk, help, is in being. When the countries became free the United States and Soviet Russia moved in with programmes of aid, tied to political and economic exploitation – the neo-colonialism. It was not surprising that as the years have passed, the leaders of the new countries have seen the value of the Commonwealth and become conscious of its potential as an association of equals. It needs a few men of vision – preferably not from Britain – to build on the foundations.

The Investiture of the Prince of Wales at Caernarvon Castle on 1 July 1969. The Prince has just knelt before the Queen and taken his oath. Over the gate of the castle are the feathers, emblem of the Princes of Wales since they were won at the Battle of Crécy in 1346.

ABOVE Reason to be pleased. Driving away from the Investiture, which was successful beyond all expectations. The Prince was 21 later in the year.

LEFT In the North-West Territories of Canada for the anniversary celebrations of 1970.

OPPOSITE ABOVE When the roses were blooming. The Queen with President Nixon and his wife and Mr Edward Heath, the then Prime Minister, in the gardens at Chequers, the PM's official country house.

OPPOSITE BELOW The difficult State Visit. Emperor Hirohito visits Britain in October 1971.

ABOVE A Thai welcome. The grace and beauty of classical dancers.

LEFT A Thai farewell. The elephants did not forget.

OPPOSITE ABOVE At Stirling University in Scotland, 1972. The visit went to the heads of some of the undergraduates . . . perhaps not just the visit.

OPPOSITE BELOW The Royal Family, 1972. Prince Charles, Prince Edward, the Queen, the Duke of Edinburgh, Prince Andrew, Princess Anne.

ABOVE The Archbishop of Canterbury, Dr Ramsey, blesses the marriage of Princess Anne and Captain Mark Phillips in Westminster Abbey on 14 November 1973.

OPPOSITE ABOVE Explaining *their* traditions during the Queen's visit to Canada in 1973.

OPPOSITE BELOW The French President, Giscard d'Estaing, on the terrace of Buckingham Palace, during a State Visit in 1976, with the black retriever given to him by the Queen. The President combines country pursuits with his intellectual activities.

The Montreal Olympic Games, 1976. The Royal Family went over in force. Princess Anne
was a member of the British Equestrian Team.
The Queen arrived with her two younger sons. Prince Charles, as heir to the throne,
does not accompany his mother on flights.

One country has been the bane of this development – South Africa. The Afrikaners were no friends to Britain when she was fighting for survival; South Africa became a republic and left the Commonwealth to pursue its policy of apartheid. Yet this helot state, through its financial links with the City of London, continues to exercise a sinister influence in Britain and embarrasses our relations with the new Africa which men such as Macmillan helped to bring to independence.

The Queen can have pride of personal achievement as she reads: 'No function attaches to the title of Head of the Commonwealth and it has no strict constitutional significance. But, as the sole symbolic link uniting all the members of the Commonwealth, it is the outward and visible mark of the special relationship which exists between them.'

The commentators have been saying for years that 'the special relationship' between Britain and the USA has ended. The inference has been that Britain should mourn this as another example of her reduced status. But, whether either country likes it or not, 'the special relationship' cannot help surviving. The Queen shows herself well aware of this in her speeches in America, especially during her visit to America in 1976 for the Bicentennial celebrations. You cannot escape the past.

From the time the Queen came to the throne until the defeat in Vietnam, the USA consciously exercised world hegemony. It is still the dominant world-power, but has accepted that it cannot run the world.

They said the British ran the world like well-intentioned schoolboys; they could say of the Americans that they ran the world like idealists whose stipends were paid by one of the multi-nationals.

Britain is firmly and willingly in the Western camp led by America. At times the USA has been heavy-handed and its overwhelming financial power has been bluntly used to influence domestic politics, but its nuclear power has preserved freedom. The price has not been too high.

The Queen has played her part in the difficult role of Anglo–Soviet relations. First courtesies, then hospitality on a larger scale have been extended. It has been a dangerous period. The key-note has been patience, hoping that with the years the drive of Soviet expansionism will lessen and the hungry missionary zeal be tempered by achievement and prosperity.

The Common Market does entail a loss of a certain sovereignty by all the member nations. But it does not entail a loss of sovereignty for the Queen. When the British finally decided to join, it was a belated justification of the life-work of Edward Heath.

For the British, great travellers and settlers beyond the oceans, have traditionally little understanding or affection for the countries across the Channel. The benefits of membership belong to the future and the squabbles for advantage in the committees of Brussels are to be preferred to the brutal arbitration of the battle-field.

The monarchy costs a considerable amount of money. But it is generally accepted that the nation's royal representative must be provided with the means to exhibit splendour on formal occasions and to give and return hospitality worthily. The Queen has struck just about the right balance. She would be unlikely to permit any close member of the family to indulge in profligate spending.

Gradually, sometimes too gradually, changes have been made in the style and manner of her officials. The greatest changes have been in the machinery for dealing with the press and TV, which was rudimentary and amateurish when she came to the throne. Without adequate publicity the monarchy could find itself fading into an agreeable, but unremarked background. There were times of great friction. But the problem has been solved as much as it probably can be solved. The appointment of professionals to the press office, and the addition of Australian and Canadian representatives have helped.

The Queen's family life has had its problems, but none of them has caused lasting damage. Prince Philip has been a devoted husband and father. The Prince of Wales has developed into a man in whom his family and the nation take pride.

The Queen has enjoyed good health and now looks better than she has ever done.

As an institution the monarchy stands secure. The criticism that arises from time to time is noticed, sometimes discussed and then fades into oblivion. Monarchy suits the British. In the Queen they have a woman who has gone about her duties, calmly and quietly and with a self-discipline that is now second nature to her.

She has worked hard, but always had time for her family and the pleasures of life. Such grief and sorrow that have come her way she has endured stoically.

Destiny called her to a great position. She has tried to be worthy of it. 'I declare before you that my whole life, whether it be long or short, shall be devoted to your service. . . .'

As for the hope of her twenty-first birthday – is the Commonwealth 'more free, more prosperous, more happy and a more powerful influence for good in the world . . .?'

The answer on the twenty-fifth anniversary of her reign is, Yes.

Index